The Eternal Mystery

The Eternal Mystery

Searching for the Creator's Thumbprint

John Sewell

Writers Club Press

San Jose New York Lincoln Shanghai

Writers Club Press
an imprint of iUniverse.com, Inc.

For information address:
iUniverse.com, Inc.
620 North 48th Street, Suite 201
Lincoln, NE 68504-3467
www.iuniverse.com

ISBN: 0-595-10054-6

Printed in the United States of America

To Mary

Epigraph

The Eternal Mystery

"The eternal mystery of the world is its comprehensibility".

A. Einstein

Contents

Preface

Why is the Bible a best-seller? Because every human being wonders about his relationship with the Eternal. Many are apprehensive and yearn for reassurance. The Bible provides that reassurance to some.

We all wonder about our origin and the origin of all we see about us. Where did it all come from? Who, or What, is responsible? The world's religions give the responsible party different names: God, Yahweh, Jehovah, Ra, Allah, The Great Spirit,—, and bestow upon him different characteristics. Most of us recognize this practice as pure conjecture, but each religion tells us we must "accept it on faith". But we are not satisfied with "faith"; we want answers supported by *evidence*. We want to know: *Is he there? Is he benign, indifferent or hostile? What are his intentions? Does he have a mission for us?*

To expect hard answers to these questions is to expect too much! But, we can look for patterns, for clues, for circumstantial evidence which may persuade us that, though, "we see through the glass, darkly", we do indeed see something!

How did I come to write this book? I have had a lifetime interest in five subjects: mathematics, science, history, the origin of Homo sapiens, and the origin of our universe. I am fascinated by the challenge of searching for the thumbprint of the Creator in those five subjects. I am, above all, fascinated by mathematics and its role in enabling both our understanding of nature and our ability to control nature. As I tell in the introduction to this book, these interests were crystallized by a statement on an MIT 'T' shirt. I decided to pursue these interests, so I wrote the book for myself.

Acknowledgements

I wish to recognize the many sources of information that I've plundered for much of the content of the book; they include ancient college text-books, the public libraries, my somewhat limited private library, friends' libraries, Science magazine, various encyclopedia, and, of course, the Internet. These are the sources of my facts; the conjectures are all mine.

It gives me great pleasure to acknowledge the support I have received from Mary Walton and Dave Dana; they reminded me of many good writing practices that I am afraid I left at the university door when I departed.

Mary, my wife and my best friend, has patiently and diligently reviewed my efforts, found errors, made valuable suggestions, and patiently put up with my musings as I searched for the thumbprint. This book is as much hers as mine.

John Sewell

Introduction

One December morning I found the following equations, "Maxwell's Equations," together with two statements, imprinted on an MIT 'T' shirt that my wife gave me for Christmas:

AND GOD SAID:

$$\nabla \times E = -\frac{\partial B}{\partial t}$$

$$\nabla \times H = \frac{\partial D}{\partial t} + i$$

$$\nabla \cdot B = 0$$

$$\nabla \cdot D = \rho$$

AND THERE WAS LIGHT
Figure 1

As I looked admiringly at the T shirt, I said to myself, "That's right! God couldn't just have said, 'Let there be light' as the Bible says, that's the **what**, and He had to deal with the **how**. He had to establish Maxwell's equations as the law of the universe". But Maxwell's equations are a mathematical statement governing the behavior of light and all other electromagnetic radiation. Does that mean that the Creator is a mathematician? Plato said he was!

As I pondered the T shirt a flood of interesting thoughts and questions raced through my mind.

As the beginning of the twenty-first century looms large in our consciences, we are constantly adding to a substantial body of knowledge about our universe. The knowledge we have gained thus far, and to which we continue to add, enables us to control our environment and to harvest from it an abundance of products of many kinds; products which enrich our lives. As we apply our mathematical and physical methods to the phenomena we see around us, we should ask, " Where does this ability to master our world come from? How does it happen that we are able to comprehend mathematics, a purely intellectual body of knowledge? *Did the Creator give us an invaluable gift of mathematical ability so that we could understand the universe?"* Other animals have the ability to understand the physical world about them well enough to form cooperative groups, feed themselves, build a nest or a den, rear their offspring, etc., but we are the only animal that deals with math. Some people would make the case that we are no more than an animal with an opposed thumb and a large brain. But we **are** more. ***We are mathematicians!***

My thoughts raced ahead. What keys to understanding the Creator's nature and intentions lay about waiting to be picked up? Are there clues of some sort to be found in the mysteries of mathematics and in the laws of nature? *Certainly the laws of nature are an expression of HIS nature.* Why is it that the micro world of the quantum mechanics of physics depends on the role of chance while the macro world is highly predictable? (Was Einstein right when he said, "I do not believe that God plays at dice with the universe?" Are the dice loaded?). Why are the secrets of the Universe revealed to us in the radiation that falls on our planet? Why is Nature so helpful and cooperative? The world of Nature promised to be one fruitful area in which to search for clues.

Why is man unique among the species? Why has he become the master of the Natural World? There is something puzzling and unsettling about the history of the New World. Why, compared to Europe and Asia, was America all but deserted until a few hundred years ago? Why did math and science flourish in Europe but not among the developed societies of North America, the Aztecs, the Mayans and the Incas? Why on three occasions (two World Wars and one Cold war) was America the key factor in preserving a world where freedom and the rule of the many was at least possible? The world of man was clearly another area in which to search for clues.

I doubted there were satisfactory answers to these and other similar questions but I believed that if I tried to explore them and formulate them more broadly I might acquire some insights that promised to be fascinating.

The Mysterious Machine

Our human experience can be compared to that of a lone traveler lost in the desert. Walking through the arid and deserted wasteland, he suddenly comes upon a huge mysterious structure, a marvelous machine. Near the structure lies a book, bound in leather and secured by a golden lock. A title is embossed on the leather: **INSTRUCTIONS FOR OPERATION AND CONTROL**. Near the book lies a golden key with a word worked into the gold; the word is **MATHEMATICS.** The key fits the lock; the traveler opens the book. He studies. He learns how to use the machine to see into the depths of space and into the depths of matter and to understand what he sees. He learns to create vast amounts of energy, to modify the very material of which he is made. His access to knowledge seems limitless. "Who built this wonder?", he asks. He searches for the answer in every corner of the structure, but there is no nameplate, no manufacturer's signature. He finds clues, but they are unfathomable and seem to obscure rather than illuminate the answer to his question. He can not find any description of the builder. He feels that the answer lies there just beyond his grasp. He does not give up. He keeps searching—. Like the structure in the desert our universe reveals to us many of its curious and mysterious physical characteristics; much of which we have learned to understand. But there is much we don't understand; we are surrounded by puzzles and enigmas. In our world, the world of man, we find curious and mysterious properties of the natural world: biotechnology, astronomy, cosmology, physics and chemistry, curious and mysterious properties of mathematics and curious and mysterious historical events. Are these mysteries only properties of nature, just what we might expect, just coincidences? There are so many arcane phenomena that the probability that chance is responsible seems very small. Is someone tinkering with the knobs; is someone trying to tell us something? Should we be looking behind these and other similar enigmas for a thread of meaning?

We are intrigued by evidence which persuades us that there is much more than chance at work in our universe; this book attempts to explore that case. Few would argue with the evidence that the universe is here because of a creative event. The Big Bang is a generally accepted theory and this theory is supported by a lot of supplementary evidence. Does Creation occur without a Creator? Why was our universe created to be so friendly? Why does the universe reveal its intimate secrets to us through the light and other electromagnetic radiation from stars, galaxies and black holes? Why have our big brains been able to understand and control so much of what surrounds us? Was it all created to be so cooperative for a reason?

We wonder about our universe: why is it so vast, why are there black holes, what is their purpose, where does the material that enters a black hole emerge? We wonder about ourselves, "Why are we here?" Are we just an accident of evolution, a chance occurrence, a result of the way in which the natural laws were established? Is our role in the cosmos "to love one another and do good works"? Do we have a future mission as a people, a role to play in some divine drama (Tragedy or Comedy)? If we have a mission, how will we learn what it is and what we must do to fulfill it?

Perhaps we are an experiment. It is hard to believe that we are the unique occupants of the universe. The universe teems with planets, billions of planets, some of which may well be sites for other similar experiments. What must we do to become a successful experiment?

If we look about we will see some very curious wrinkles in the tapestry of which we are a part; let us take a few moments to look at these and ask some fundamental questions as we gaze. If, indeed, there is a Creator, what is his nature? Is he benign, indifferent or hostile? Is it possible that he has chosen to reveal part of his nature if we are perceptive enough to look for clues and keys and to unlock some doors? Perhaps we don't need to look for "miracles" such as Paul believed he experienced on the road to Damascus or the spectacle of Lazarus rising from his grave; if we look, more subtle and more convincing miracles may confront us—but, then again, maybe not. Let's take a look.

Is there a Creator? We don't know! We know there was a creative event because there is physical evidence of the Big Bang, but, conceivably, the creative event might have been spontaneous or associated with the catastrophic event of the demise of the Supreme Being! Remember the "God is dead!" cult of a few years ago? It is a premise of this book that, as you read this, there may be a Creator at work in our universe. We are searching for evidence that might sustain or refute that premise. Will all of the evidence be circumstantial or will some of the evidence be more convincing?

Well, if we suspect that there is a Creator who may be revealing to us keys to understanding the universe, why? Some might answer: "Perhaps the Creator wants to assure our future, to have us achieve the goals he wants us to achieve." But many of us will reject this thought, for we have "free will" in the classical sense (the power to make our own choices without divine interference). In the application of our scientific discoveries we have the option of survival or extinction in our own hands. Nowhere is this more obvious than in the consequences of the discovery of nuclear energy; will it be nature's greatest gift to an energy-hungry world or will we find in it the means for self-annihilation?

Many of the philosophers and authors who have enriched our human culture have seen in our world the classic struggle between Good and Evil; the struggle flourishes today in the ethnic conflicts which abound in Africa, Europe and Asia. Will some sort of ultimate enlightenment resolve this struggle in favor of Good, or will Evil triumph? If the Creator cares about the outcome, why should he care? Why should **we** care? After all, every inhabitant of the planet two centuries hence will be a stranger to us. We will be gone. Why should we care whether or not these people of the future find their lives as we have found ours? Why? But we do care, don't we!

In the depths of his being man chooses to believe that the Creator cares even if he does not directly interfere; man chooses to believe, based on the evidence of which I shall write, that there may be a benign influence at work in our lives. But is this belief a rational choice or an emotional one; is there really any evidence of that benign hand influencing our affairs to our benefit, or is it just wishful thinking? Let the reader decide!

The Search for Clues

This is a book written for people who want to search for clues to a great philosophical mystery: our relationship with the eternal (if there is one). What evidence might convince us that there is a watchful eye and a careful hand guiding the evolution of our species? Or that there is not? In the past three hundred years Nature has yielded up many of her secrets to us, to genus Homo sapiens; is this revelation an accident or is it something more? The book asks some profound questions and has few answers, but perhaps, as each reader ponders the material, he or she will acquire some insights of their own into this complex riddle.

Those who look to the Bible for clues are looking at the experiences and opinions of inhabitants of our planet who lived several thousand years ago. Our ancient forebears knew almost nothing of the laws of nature; they saw in unusual natural events evidence of the interference of the Almighty in the affairs of men. For the most part, the Almighty was punishing his children for their misdeeds. Great significance was attributed to dreams. Dreams were the vehicle the Almighty used to guide his believers. The biblical authors were convinced that they had been granted revelations from the Supreme Being, and who is to say they had not? But we shall look at discoveries made by our fellow men: revelations about our evolution as a species and revelations in the form of natural laws that enable us to predict how nature will behave in the future. The consequences of these laws are reproducible as we choose to perform experiments and to employ them in our machines, in our health care, and elsewhere.

Where shall we look for clues? Where might we find the hand-print of a subtle, watchful and, perhaps, benign hand?

We shall begin by looking for clues in some remarkable events in man's developmental history. There is evidence that there were some sudden surges in the size and capability of the human brain. There was a sudden migratory surge out of Africa that populated Europe, Asia, and Australia, but it was not until very much later that man found his way to the New World. There were sudden advances in Homo sapien's ability to communicate. Man learned to tally, then to count, then to explore the properties of numbers, then to begin to experiment with nature in order to predict nature's future behavior.

We shall look for clues in the natural world. Here, again, there are sudden surges, surges in man's understanding of nature. There was a flowering of knowledge in ancient Greece followed by two thousand years of darkness. Then the seventeenth century saw a remarkable explosion of knowledge about mathematics and about the laws of nature. At the turn of the twenty-first century, we are now in the fortunate position of knowing a lot about how nature works. We are a long way from knowing everything, but we know a great deal! If we are to look at nature and understand what we see we must look through the eyes of the physicist, the chemist, the biochemist and the cosmologist. For many readers a list of these scientific subjects will conjure up unpleasant memories of encounters with science in high school. For those who have chosen to forget or are unfamiliar with these sciences, keep an open mind and be not apprehensive; we shall explain as we go along. We shall make a limited exploration of a fascinating world, full of surprises and beauty. With a little effort all will become clear. We shall not require any problem solving by the reader; that's a promise!

We shall look for clues in the world of mathematics. Why does much of this book focus on math?

Because mathematics enables us to understand the natural world, not vice-versa. The natural world does not enable us to understand mathematics!

In order for us to explore the mysteries of the natural world we must have some familiarity with numbers and mathematics; they are the key to understanding and controlling nature. It is mathematics that enables us to unravel the mysteries of the natural laws, to design complex machines and to conduct sophisticated commerce and finance. Mathematics is the means by which scientists communicate with each other; it is their universal language. **Without mathematics we would be living as our primitive ancestors lived!**

Except for professionals who apply some math in their daily work, many readers will have forgotten, or at least will have permitted to become rusty, what they learned in school, so there is a little review in what follows. There are many examples that are intended to resurrect mathematical knowledge and spark the interest of the reader. And most of us never encountered in school some of the fascinating material we will consider on this journey.

Mathematics blazes the trail we shall follow; math is the foundation of our ability to understand not only nature in all its variety: physics, chemistry, biology, geology, and astronomy, but also cosmology and our universe. Math is not only the means by which we understand and control the natural world, but math has "other-worldly" properties. It is not part of the "real world" (although its applications are); it is constructed of man's discoveries in an unreal world and thus it is a hunting-ground for mysteries "in the abstract".

Consequently, a broad mathematical ribbon runs through the book. The reader may need to resurrect some forgotten skills, but there is nothing beyond any reader's comprehension and there are fascinating relationships buried in the numbers that will astound him or her. We will pause to examine numbers and their mysterious, curious, and thought-provoking properties, but we will not embrace the mysticism and pseudo-science of numerology.

Regrettably, there are times and places in this book where it is necessary to resort to some mathematical jargon, but if we are to talk about math we have no choice but to call the math things by their right names. The author does his best to define these terms and give examples that clarify them, and there is a Glossary of Terms to which the reader may refer if his memory fails to record what he has encountered in the text. If you make the effort to understand we shall both succeed. For those who wish further enlightenment about the math issues addressed in the text there are several appendices.

As we travel this mathematical highway we will meet others who have traveled this road before us: Primitive Man, Pythagoras, Euclid, Galileo, Fermat, Maxwell, Einstein and others. We may pause briefly to become acquainted with them, to see them in the milieu in which they discovered those foundation blocks on which we build today. We shall try to see them not only as geniuses, but also as fellow humans. The great Einstein, discoverer of Special and General Relativity, exhibited considerable appeal to the ladies!

The road ahead is interesting in itself because we will pass some scenery that is very curious and which will remind us that math has many mysterious properties. Occasionally we will make a few detours to explore interesting byways. What we encounter along the road may make us pause to entertain some speculations that are fascinating and provocative.

We shall search for clues in human history. We shall speculate about our prehistory, about the world-view of our primitive ancestors. Before the appearance of us Homo sapiens the primitive world was populated by Homo erectus; a genus from which Homo sapiens emerged. We know very little about Homo erectus or the first Homo sapiens; our speculation is based on sparse archaeological and anthropological knowledge. Apart from finds of ancient human bones, an occasional footprint in hardened mud, or teeth marks on the bones of animals which provided dinner to our predecessors there is little or nothing to tell us about them or their life styles. Then as relics from the past: structures, primitive tools, pottery and, later, recorded history become available to us, we shall be able to be more confident of the events we discuss. When we arrive at what may be called the modern period, the period that begins with the Greek philosophers, we shall follow man's progress in his discoveries of the structure of our world and the natural laws which govern its behavior.

Man's intellectual development was the key to his discoveries in the worlds of math and science, consequently the structure of the book is generally chronological and the two subjects are interwoven throughout the text. Occasionally it will contribute to the reader's understanding if we abandon a rigorous adherence to chronology, retrace our steps a little way, introduce a new subject, and then continue to forge ahead. But first a few words about historical perspective.

Historical Perspective

Our society is plagued with a distorted perception of historical time; we view even our recent ancestors as occupants of a distant past. They are not. As we explore the history of our predecessors and their acquisition of knowledge about mathematics and nature we are going to be looking in the rearview mirror of time. What we see in that mirror, and what we make of what we see, will depend on our perspective. Let's look at our ancestors carefully, as fellow humans, who differ from us only in the abundant knowledge that is ours.

We see the founders of our country as ancients; nothing could be more mistaken. To be sure, they wore wigs and strange clothing, knee britches and shoes with buckles. George Washington had wooden teeth. The tools and machinery of the early settlers of the United States were very crude.

The inhabitants of Europe were equally strange. But we are less than a tick of the historical clock from these contemporary humans.

Our judgement of historical timescale is impaired by the influence of rapidly accelerating progress in science, engineering, technology—the whole body of knowledge—and the corresponding transformation of transportation, communication, health and agriculture. At the time of Thomas Jefferson, less than 200 years ago, the means of transportation were by foot, by horse and by water. That was it, period. Was that a long time ago? Not at all! It just seems like a long time because our perspective is warped by Jefferson's lack of all the sophisticated tools and comforts we enjoy today. He wasn't different, he was deprived!

Jefferson's ancestors did not live much differently than he, even those that preceded him by several thousand years. Same transportation by foot and by horse, same society based on slave labor, almost the same primitive agriculture, almost the same wind-driven water transportation. Man's lifestyle had changed but little from the time of the enormous transformation from hunter-gatherers to a farming society, and that happened many thousand years ago.

Only a little more than 100 years ago there were no airplanes; the horseless carriage, telephones and electric lighting were a curiosity and unavailable to most people. Many steamships were still assisted by sails and city streets abounded with the fragrance of horse manure. Our great-grandparents inhabited this antiquated world; it is only a short step behind us.

In terms of intelligence, in the sense of genetic capabilities, we citizens of the twenty-first century probably differ but little from the people who inhabited the Fertile Crescent ten thousand years ago; in terms of knowledge the gulf is enormous. So, as we explore the evolution of physical and mathematical knowledge, let us think of the people who made the mathematical and scientific discoveries, and applied them to practical problems, as our contemporaries.. Indeed, they are our contemporaries in every respect except for the fund of knowledge available to them.

As we proceed with our search we shall look at many mysteries, discoveries and inventions. We all know what a mystery is, but how does one distinguish between discovery and invention? In this book we shall define a discovery as the uncovering of new knowledge about nature or mathematics; invention will be defined as assembling existing knowledge of nature to achieve a new application. We shall not be very rigorous in deciding which is which; there are more than enough of each to go around. When we reach the end of our journey, and if the author has successfully done what he set out to do, the reader will put this book aside, ponder the origin, the source, of what we humans have learned about our world and wonder—. Are we humans solely responsible for what we now know or—?

We begin at the beginning, with a mix of fact and conjecture about our origin, the origin of genus Homo sapiens. There is a marvelous conjecture about our ancestry which may alter the way in which the reader looks at his fellows.

Chapter One

Where Did We Homo Sapiens Come from?

There is an interesting and intriguing theory, or perhaps a better term is conjecture, among anthropologists regarding our ancestry. It is not a theory accepted by all, but the evidence in support of the theory is very powerful. The theory is that every human on the planet has one common ancestor, a woman who lived in Africa perhaps 5000 generations ago, a woman whom we all must call Great Great Grandmother. For obvious reasons she has been named The Mother of Us All by her anthropological descendants and Eve by the media. (How did the author of Genesis know about her?) Before we pursue the fascinating story of Eve, let us set the stage for the appearance of "us" Homo sapiens and our ascendancy among the species on the planet.

There is reasonably convincing evidence that "modern man", our species, Homo sapiens, first appeared on the planet between 90,000 and 200,000 years ago somewhere in eastern/southern Africa. Homo sapiens split off from an evolutionary species known broadly as Homo erectus, a term which persuades us that Homo erectus was a biped not a quadruped. Homo erectus appeared nearly two million years ago and his ancestors evolved from the apes millions of years earlier. Homo erectus evolved into a number of sub-species all of which, according to the Eve conjecture, are now extinct (except, of course, for us Homo sapiens). In the period beginning perhaps a million years ago these Homo erectus derivatives had emerged from Africa and had populated Europe and Asia. Peking man, Java man, Neanderthal man, all of these were members of Homo erectus. Color them gone.

By definition of the word "species", the members of one species are not able to breed with another species and produce viable offspring. A horse and a donkey, two different species, can breed and produce an offspring, a mule, but the mule is unable to reproduce, a mule is not a member of a species. It is clear, based on the evidence provided by skeletons and bones, that Homo sapiens and his Homo erectus cousins occupied the planet at the same time, but only Homo sapiens survived. If Homo sapiens and Homo erectus were indeed different species, then Homo sapiens is here, Homo erectus is gone, and nary a single Homo erectus gene resides in us today. However, some anthropologists believe that the two Homos were indeed able to breed and that the genetic influence of Java man, Peking man, and Neanderthal man is to be found in modern humans. Unfortunately, there is no evidence which is sufficiently clear that it can settle the debate.

If we examine the skeletal remains of Neanderthals, for example, they are different from us, but the differences seem to be ones of detail. As we look at their skulls we see that their brows are lower, their jaws heavier, the brain cavity smaller, the chin less prominent and the eyes set closer to the top of the skull. From their skeletons we see that they were powerfully built. Could our ancestors have bred successfully with these creatures? Our DNA differs but little from the DNA of chimps (chimps and Homo sapiens share the same DNA characteristics at the 98-99 percent level) and yet the differences between the chimps and our human species are very great indeed. The DNA's of horse and donkey probably differ very little and yet they can not produce viable offspring; it seems quite credible that our ancestors and the Neanderthals may well have been likewise.

Why did our ancestors prevail over the Homo erectus Neanderthals? Why did the Neanderthals disappear? We see animal species with far less capability than the Neanderthals thriving; why did not the two species survive together as two different species of humans? In fact, is it not strange that there is no "nearby" species to man, especially when there were several different species of Homo erectus?

Neanderthal remains were first discovered near Dusseldorf in Germany, at a rather high latitude, so Neanderthals must have found a way to survive the rigors of the great sheets of ice that covered much of Europe during the Pleistocene period. They were survivors! Why are they gone? Did our ancestors eliminate them in a bloody struggle, or were they victims of a declining birth rate or some genetic disorder that finally finished them? Let us say that Homo sapiens was superior and the Neanderthals inferior, but that is not reason enough to explain their extinction. We are superior to the chimps and yet they are not extinct. In any event, the Neanderthals are gone, we are here, and we may have one woman, Eve, to thank for it.

But what about Eve? What evidence is there to support the claim that she is our Granny? In the nucleus of every cell in our body is to be found an extremely complex system of chromosomes and long strings of DNA (a very long molecule) associated with each chromosome. The chromosomes number 23 and come in pairs. The members of each pair are not dramatically different from each other in the female, and 22 of the 23 are not dramatically different in the male, but the 23'd pair in the male differ from each other very significantly; they have been designated X and Y respectively. When sexual reproduction takes place the pairs split into two sets; one of the female's sets joins with one of the male's sets to form the new chromosomal pairs and a new life begins. The new life carries the mother's characteristics from her set of chromosomes and likewise for the father. If the union carries the Y it will be a boy, if not, a girl.

Each DNA molecule is composed of a series of genes in a long line, an enormous number of genes that makes each of us unique. Each gene is a long, coded message the letters of which are formed by "amino acids". The number of permutations and combinations in a gene is astronomical! The chromosomes are found in the cell nucleus and are passed to each of us half by our father and half by our mother.

But outside the cell nucleus, in the fluid material that surrounds the nucleus, in the cytoplasm, are found the mitochondria. The mitochondria are very tiny structures which play a role in metabolic (energy production) processes in the body. The mitochondria also has a complement of DNA, but it is far simpler than that of the nucleus; it consists of only 37 genes. It has been proven that the mitochondrial DNA is passed only from mother to child; furthermore, the female children can pass it on to their offspring, but the male children can not. Consequently, there are special female-to-female DNA links in the genealogical chain consisting of mother to female child. Each female child is the mother passing to the next link in the chain, her female offspring.

In the early nineties a group of researchers at UC Berkeley examined the placenta from over 100 women drawn from African, Asian, European, and Australian aboriginal groups. The commonality of the mitochondrial DNA was unmistakable, the women in the sample all had a common ancestor! We are ALL brothers and sisters under the skin! Differences in skin pigmentation and physical features are probably due to differences in diet, climate and to the relative isolation of what are now different ethnic groups. So, the next time you see another person whom you find either magnetically attractive or horribly repulsive, remember, he or she is a relative!

Accompanying the Eve story is an extraordinary, and probably largely successful, attempt to time her appearance and to establish the geographical location at which she resided. How was this done? Scientists have established that the remarkable reproduction of cells in our bodies proceeds with remarkable reliability; there is seldom a mistake; cells we reproduce are identical to the parent cell. Almost always, but not always. Occasionally there is a mutation, a cell makes a mistake and creates a cell which has different characteristics. One of the pairs of amino acids in the gene has experienced a substitution. It is this process of mutation combined with natural selection that accounts for evolution of the various species. Perhaps the cell has been struck by a cosmic ray, has had an unusual encounter with some chemical agent, or has experienced a trauma of some sort; whatever the cause, it is different. Then that deviant cell reproduces. The new cell may be beneficial to the organism of which it is a part, and, in that case, there is a strong probability that the mutant strain of cells will survive. The new cell may be unfavorable to its organism in which case it may not survive, as natural selection does its job to weed out the weakest and preserve the fittest. Often the mutation may be more or less neutral, neither favorable nor unfavorable to its organism, and in that case it is likely to survive. In the case of mitochondrial DNA the rate at which mutations occur, although the mutations are random, is, averaged over a long time, relatively constant, and is of the order of two to four percent in one million years.

Now, suppose that one family of children splits into two groups, group A and group B, each group containing females which will reproduce. Both groups A and B have a common female ancestor, their mother, and share a common mitochondrial DNA. The gene mutations that the individuals in the two groups (and their string of offspring) experience will, of course, be different. By comparing the mitochondrial DNA of the descendants of the two groups the differences in the number of gene mutations will establish how long a time has elapsed since they shared a common ancestor. Or, perhaps to put it more accurately, how long a time has elapsed since the divergence from a single common gene. In this way the appearance of the ancestral gene (Eve) has been established at about 90,000 to 200,000 years ago. Using the same technique, it has been established that she almost undoubtedly existed in Africa.

How about Adam, or Adams? Is it likely that the society in which Eve lived was monogamous? Even to those sophisticated Europeans who were the cream of the 19th century social scene the term monogamous was a subject for riotous laughter; they were promiscuous at every opportunity. Who would expect more circumspect behavior of Eve and her companions? Eve's contemporaries were in all probability naked, self-centered, taking what they wanted from their fellows, and sexually promiscuous.

What was the size of the population pool of which Eve was a part? It was probably relatively large, perhaps numbering many tens of thousands. In terms of our nuclear DNA Eve's DNA is a miniscule part because the gene code gets revised every time the male and female chromosomes do their tango; buried in our DNA are the gifts from many of her contemporaries.

But none of this detracts from the astonishing fact that we can all trace our genealogy back to one common female ancestor! Is this just an incredible accident or did Eve have such important gifts that they were essential to Homo sapiens' future?

What was so special about Eve, about her mitochondrial DNA, that her line should survive while all those outside her line disappear? She was one member of a moderately numerous primitive population pool. Nearly all of the other female members of that pool must have reproduced; what happened that their lines should die out? Today Eve's DNA resides in every one of us humans, us Homo sapiens. In every cell in our bodies Eve's DNA is at work in the mitochondria providing the cell with the energy it needs to function. Is that strange or what?

Based on the facts, one must conclude that Eve's DNA conferred upon her line special abilities of a profound nature. All the competitors failed! These special mitochondrial-based abilities were passed on by the females alone; the fathers can not pass it on. Perhaps Eve's line made better tools, had some special physical characteristics, better vision, better hearing, better cognitive abilities; since, whatever it was, we all have it, there is no way to differentiate among today's populations.

At least as impressive as the Eve story is the disappearance of the Neanderthals and their cousins in the rest of the land masses of Europe, Asia and Africa. It is astounding that today there is no living remnant of these millions of humans! The dinosaurs disappeared, we believe today, because their food supply was erased by a huge meteor that collided with our planet, and threw up a cloud of dust and debris into the global atmosphere. The dust cloud interrupted the solar energy which nourished the vegetation on which the dinosaurs fed. And the spotted owl's localized and endangered habitat may eliminate his species. But the derivatives of Homo erectus were scattered over continents, enjoyed a wide variety of habitat and diet and had survived for millions of years.

Why? Why are they gone? Many species with less obvious survival skills are here today: horses, chimps, spotted owls—what happened to our fellows the Neanderthals? Did some mystical hand decide to color them gone in order that Homo sapiens should prevail?

Did evolution arrange the passage of mitochondrial DNA from mother to child in such a way that only daughters could pass it on? If so, why? What is the significance of this curious fact? Is this odd characteristic unique to humans, Homo sapiens, or do other species exhibit the same quality? What of the Neanderthal species?

There are many strange and puzzling features to this story, features that may make us suspect intervention. Is our path through the corridors of time being guided in some subtle way that we can not really identify but for which there are elusive clues that perplex us? Who is the guide, what is the path, and what is the destination?

The path is clearer than the source of guidance; the path is knowledge. We are being swept forward on a stream, now a river, a torrent, of knowledge. Our knowledge about ourselves and our world is increasing at an exponential rate. Where does the path end? Is there an end? If there is an end, what is our destiny? Will we, like the Neanderthals, just disappear, or do we have a mission to perform?

Chapter Two

The Dawn of Man

Let's try to imagine the world-view of a very primitive Homo sapiens, one of us, a man who lived 100,000 or more years ago. At that time the world was populated by Homo erectus with whom Homo sapiens coexisted. Homo erectus was to be found in Africa, Asia and, possibly, Australia; he walked on two legs and survived by hunting and gathering wild plants and vegetables. Our genus, Homo sapiens, split off from the Homo erectus stem.

At the center of his world Homo sapiens finds himself. Beyond that center is everything else. It is an **I-Everything Else** view; a twofold universe. In the **Everything Else** part of that universe were other humans, Homo sapiens, Homo erectus, and animals, vegetables and minerals, but they were all part of a whole in the sense that they were not **He**. As he evolved, the **Everything Else** separated into *Other Homo sapiens* and *Everything Else*; now *Everything Else* was different from the former **Everything Else**, it was less inclusive. It included animals, vegetables and minerals but not the other creatures who were like himself. Now the universe was *I-You-Other*, a threefold universe. The *Yous* were his fellows; it was clear to him that they were a special class, distinct from the animals and inanimate objects that surrounded him. He and his fellows shared a cave, food from the hunt and the warmth of a community fire. He didn't understand the quantities two (or three) in the numerical way that we do, these concepts were still far in the future.

Oneness was the fundamental part of his existence, for **He** was the **One** His world did indeed revolve around himself, around his needs for food and shelter, around his survival in a hostile world. But twoness was beginning to intrude. Day or Night, Rain or Shine, Feast or Famine, Male or Female, Dead or Alive, Man and Mate; a dichotomy dominated the essential features of the world beyond his oneness. Twoness came to his consciousness: two eyes, two ears, two hands, two legs. Beyond one, two is the giant of the numbers because it relates to so many of our everyday experiences and because it is the beginning of the progression to the whole set of numbers. Without two there would be no three, four, five...

Intruding into the twofold world surrounding our ancestor came a child to himself and his mate, *I-mate-child*, and then *I-mate-children*. He was not equipped to make a numerical distinction between the world with a single child compared to a world with several. More generally, there was a plurality beyond the *I-you*, beyond those who were like himself, a plurality which included animals, trees, mountains. The plurality required a distinction.

The distinction was made with names, just as the distinction among his fellows was made with names. (This may well be the way in which languages were born). So, the many features of our ancestor's world were not indistinguishable from one another; the names took care of that, but until the discovery of tallying there was no one-to-one correspondence with another set of objects. There was no consciousness of an identifiable quantitative difference, the kind of difference we would describe as a **numerical** difference. There was only the *Many*.

Never-the-less the seeds leading to twoness, threeness and counting had been planted. The first seed to sprout was tallying. But before we get to tallying we need to follow the progress of our Homo sapien ancestors as they emerged from Africa and occupied Europe, Asia and Australia.

Something Happened to Us on the Way to the Ice Age!

Something very remarkable happened to Homo sapiens about 50,000 years ago. Suddenly, after millennia of slow evolutionary progress, there was an explosion! The explosion came not in one area of human existence but in many. As we look through the cloudy lens of archaeology it appears that the explosion in these various areas came almost simultaneously, (at least where a thousand years is the unit of time). We see the emergence of complex language, symbolism, art, agriculture, animal husbandry, and a great migration out of Africa into Europe, Asia minor, Asia, and Australia. Why? Why did our evolutionary rate take a sudden and spectacular turn upward? Why did our ancestors decide to abandon Africa and spread out over the land mass accessible to them? Were they pushed?

Anatomically, hominids were ready to speak 150,000 years ago; the throat (larynx) and tongue had evolved to their present condition and were capable of forming the necessary sounds, and, no doubt, there was some crude communication. Those who have seen "The Quest For Fire" or Raquel Welsh in "1000 Years BC" are acquainted with Hollywood's version of the grunts and monosyllables used by our predecessors as well as the incendiary couture of the Cave Lassies. And who is to say that Hollywood is wrong since none of the actual real sounds used to communicate have left a record, there are no sound fossils! But there is a big chasm between rudimentary communication and a complex language. Language seems to have first appeared about 50,000 years ago. Rather suddenly, in the opinion of many archaeologists, although there is a contrary opinion held by some. These doubters believe that language developed over a long period of time as the social and cultural environment of our ancestors grew together with the growth of populations and a tendency of people to cluster together.

Why did language appear so recently in the long history of man's development? It is unlikely that it was the result of a lack of brain power.

There is physiological evidence that for a million and a half years our ancestors experienced gradual brain growth from a small brain, the size of our ancestral chimp's, to about 900 cubic centimeters (a little more than half of what most of us have today). Then about 500,000 years ago there was a more or less sudden inflation to today's 1500 cc. What accounts for this burst of increase in brain capacity? Some believe there was a lucky mutation that triggered this fortunate change; others believe it was a consequence of the growth of population and the social interaction that went hand-in-hand with it. The inflation was accompanied by a change in brain structure that significantly enlarged the frontal and temporal lobes of the brain; these are the areas where much of our ability to think creatively and to verbalize those thoughts takes place. So no doubt the ability to develop a complex language was resident in our species long before the appearance of the evidence for such speech.

Whatever the source of the development of language it is certain that it was accompanied by both the use of symbols and also the pictorial representation of symbols, which most of us would call "art". There was an explosion of Ice Age art in Europe about 40,000 years ago. Most of us have seen photographs of the marvelous lifelike drawings and paintings of animals on the walls of the deep French caves. This cave-art is believed to be about 35,000 years old as established by carbon dating techniques. The paintings are truly awesome, for they capture the wild look of horses and the fearsome appearance of mammoths, wild boars, large cats and so on. Picasso could have done no better! Other art objects include skillfully carved figurines of stone and ivory, beads and pierced teeth that must have been worn as decoration. There are extensive deposits of a red pigment called ochre to be found all over Europe and also as far away as Australia where ochre crayons were discovered. Did the ancestral distaff aborigines invent lipstick?

Art requires social interaction; how did communities originate, and why? Until recently archaeologists believed that communities, i.e. villages, arose as a consequence of agricultural development, but now there is evidence that sizeable, even large, communities appeared before there was significant agricultural activity. Why did these people gather together? The most probable causes proposed are: extended family groups, religion, culture, defense and cooperative hunts and gathering expeditions, but the supporting evidence is slim.

There is a large dig going on in Turkey at a location called Catalhoyuk. The community that prospered there 9,000 years ago numbered as many as 10,000 souls! The reason is a mystery, but the houses were jammed together in the midst of an open area. Over time, house accumulated upon house, layer upon layer, twelve layers deep, with a resulting mound about sixty feet high! The dead were buried under the floors of the houses, and on the house walls are impressive murals depicting hunts and other aspects of life as it was then experienced and, we hope, enjoyed. The community appears to have existed by hunting game and gathering wild plants for their tables. It seems that there were extended family groups living close together with little interaction with neighboring families. Why did all of these people cluster together? It is almost certainly not because of agriculture, and there is little evidence of shared labor, which is characteristic of people in cities. Catalhoyuk was not a city; no public buildings have been discovered to date, although much excavation remains. Why were all those people there?

Now that our ancestors had enlarged brains they put them to work. At first they supplemented their hunting and gathering activities with tending wild plants; then they considered their environment, did some crude analysis and selectively exploited whatever nature had endowed their habitat with. They domesticated cereal grains, rye in the Middle East, rice in China. They practiced animal husbandry, domesticating first sheep then cattle. They gathered together in cooperative groups, shared labor, developed religious practices, built cities with public buildings and a hierarchy of social strata—kings, priests, soldiers, scribes, and ultimately a leisure class.

The period between 50,000 and 10,000 years ago saw an explosive development of Homo sapiens. It began with the migration out of Africa and the occupation of the European, Asian, and Australian continents; it was accompanied by the disappearance of the Neanderthals, the development of complex language, tools, the first stirrings of numbers and mathematics, art, multiple religions, and the growth of enormous populations. Why did this dramatic and benign change in the evolutionary pattern occur? Was it just an accident, a chance mutation? There are those who will say, "It was the increase of population density, or the development of language". No doubt those are part of the mechanism, but what was the cause of the explosion? Why was there this sudden deviation in the pattern of ancient life? What, or *Who*, was responsible?

Recorded History

Recorded history begins only rather recently, about 10,000 years ago. It is recorded in artifacts; in a few sparse remains of societies that existed at that time. Some of those remains tell us a little about Homo sapiens's efforts to improve his mathematical abilities.

In order to pursue the search for the keys and clues which are the subject of this book we need to have some understanding of the tools that permit us to analyze the world about us and assign causes to what we see and experience. These tools are mathematics and the physical sciences. **Without mathematics there would be no physical sciences; without the physical sciences there would be no civilization as we know it!** In order to understand how our civilization evolved we must review the way in which those tools accumulated in the toolbox. The first of these tools was tallying. Tallying is a very primitive tool, but it marked a giant step forward in the development of mathematics.

Tallying

The very beginning of "mathematics" was tallying. Before they learned to tally, people probably kept track of each other and of domestic animals by name. We still do that; all our brothers and sisters, pets and domestic animals, as long as their number is not too large, have names. We keep track of them by name, not by number. "Where is Joe?" not "Where is number 6?". And if someone is missing from the family, or a horse from the stable, we recognize their absence as a missing element of a familiar group, not by the diminution of a number, a total.

At some point the quantity of people or of animals or of familiar articles becomes too large for us to keep track of by name, and the next step is tallying. A tally creates a one-to-one correspondence between a group of articles and a row of beans, or a row of sticks, or a row of pebbles. The number of tally-items is the same as the number of articles. But tallying becomes very cumbersome, and error-prone, for large quantities, and an improved method becomes essential. Our ancestor needed the ability to keep account of items more effectively, he needed numbers, but the numbers were a long time in coming.

Before our ancestors had the ability to count with numbers, large groups of people or other items were probably described as "many" or "very many". A handful of people or items were described by "a few". How many stars in the heavens? Many, many! That question receives the same answer today "many, many" stars, for they are not countable. (Indeed, the number of galaxies, each of which contains billions of stars, has been estimated recently at 50 billion!). Undoubtedly tallying led to "more than", "less than" and "the same" (equal to) when our ancestor compared his tally to the articles it represented. These same designations are extensively employed today in the mathematics used by our digital computers.

Primitive man's first "mathematical" challenge must have been keeping track of the family possessions, tallying a few precious items: skins of animals the family used for clothing and bedding, cooking utensils, gourds for storing water, stone tools; small numbers of items for which he could find a one to one correspondence with a row of nuts, beans (the first bean-counters!) or knots on a string. Then, as his possessions became more numerous, the large quantity of nuts or knots became more cumbersome so he added another row to his tally, probably of a different kind of counters, say pebbles. Each pebble in the second row equaled the total number of beans in the first row, and his tallying became manageable again, but he had no names nor any symbols for any of the quantities he dealt with.

We follow the same practice today, but we have names for the rows of pebbles (columns of numbers for us); as we add up a dozen or so large figures. The first column of numbers (last on the right) is the set of units, zero to nine, the second column the set of tens, next the hundreds, thousands etc. with as many columns as necessary. Notice that each of these systems employs a place-value. The pebbles in the second row have a greater value than the beans in the first row. Likewise, the numbers in the second of our columns have a value ten times that of the first (units) column. The concept of *place value* simplified arithmetic enormously.

Several thousand years ago there were ancestors whose mathematical instincts were focused on tallying. Fortunately, they left us some records of their methods of keeping track of possessions. The earliest artifacts discovered to date that deal with tallying are about 8,000 to 10,000 years old, but there were probably crude tallies long before that. The earliest mathematical records of progress beyond tallying are really very recent in the grand scheme of things, dating from about 6,000 years ago (4,000 BC).

Tallying is not counting. Tallying is the process of setting up a one-to-one correspondence between one set of articles and another set of different articles without identifying each with a number. A set of six apples is represented by a set of six sticks, this is tallying.

(Counting associates a number, a word or a symbol, with each of a series of articles. Enumerating the articles enables one to arrive at a total. One is a number-word, 1 is a number symbol. Before there were number symbols there were number-words. Six apples may be individually represented by words: number one, number two, three, four, five, and six, or by symbols: 1,2,3,4,5,6. This is enumeration or counting. Unlike tallying, each apple has a unique identifier.)

As he became more adept at tallying, primitive man recognized that a one-to-one correspondence applied not only to one set of similar articles, to other humans, to animals or birds, fishes, fellow tribesmen, stone axes, but also to a mix of articles, to whatever needed tallying. His tally could include all the trophies of a hunt: one antelope, one boar, three birds and six fishes for a total tally of eleven. And it was very convenient to use the fingers as tallying devices.

We use our hands even today as tallying aids; do you know how to use your knuckles to help remember which months have 31 days? Start with the knuckle on your index finger, that is January. February is the valley between index and middle knuckle, March, May and July are the next knuckles, intervening months in the valleys. July, then, is the knuckle of the little finger; so is August. Now we count backward with September the valley between little and ring fingers; October and December are the next two knuckles; we end on the middle knuckle. All knuckles are 31-day months, all valleys 30 (or 28). There is a one-to-one correspondence between knuckles and one kind of months, and between valleys and another kind of months, a form of tallying!

One of the earliest recovered tallying relics, a bone tool-handle found in Zaire and estimated at 10,000 years old, shows columns of notches, purpose unknown, but without doubt the notcher was setting up a one-to-one correspondence with some set of articles. Each notch represented one of the articles, not a specific one, in other words, *an* article. The articles may have been cows or other animals, people, sacks of grain or enemies killed in battle, or a mix of such things.

Let's suppose each notch represented a sack of grain. The ancient accountant had no numbers to work with and no ability to "count" the number of sacks. In the morning he could not verify the sack-count, for he knew no numbers, but he would compare the members of the pile of grain sacks to the quantity of notches to see if any sacks had been stolen during the night. He would know because he had a tally. See Figure 2.

///// ///// ///// ///// //

Figure 2

That's the way we tally today, for the most part, one stroke for each item in the tally, but there are other more colorful tallies. A fighter pilot paints the image of an airplane on his fighter aircraft fuselage for each kill; a bomb near a bomber's nose tallies each bombing mission. Only yesterday it was notches on the old six shooter tallying the number of other bad guys the gunman had guided to the next world. Are you old enough to remember Harry Belafonte, "Hey Mr. Tallyman tally me banana?" Tallying is with us today, big-time.

The tally of Figure 2 also shows the concept of grouping. The tally is done by groups of five, and when the tally is complete, the number of items can be determined by *counting* the number of groups, adding the groups by fives (multiplying by five), and adding any single tally marks that form a group less than five. Grouping is found on ancient tallysticks, often in groups of five notches, and sometimes several groups of five are separated by a long notch on the tallystick.

Why do we tally in groups of five? Because people have five fingers on each hand. Or more accurately, four fingers and a thumb! From two hands we have ten fingers and with ten toes a total of twenty. These numbers figure very prominently in the assignment of names and symbols in various number systems: Roman (five, ten), French (twenty), Indian (ten) and so on. Grouping led to the establishment of bases. Ancient number systems in different societies used different bases; some systems were based on five, some on ten, some on twenty and some on sixty. Relics of these various systems survive today; how many seconds in a minute, how many minutes in an hour? Meet an ancient sexagesimal (60) based system. We are not yet completely immersed in a number system based on ten!

Eventually there was a transition from tallying to the use of numbers. The availability of numbers led to counting. Mathematics is not counting, but, as we shall see, one of the roles of mathematics is determining if some sets of numbers are countable!

Chapter Three

The Discovery of Numbers, Language and Writing

Numbers

In addition to his first awareness of twoness, primitive man must have been conscious of pairing, a special case of twoness: man and mate, a hunter and his companion, a male and female bird sharing a nest and pairs of animals. His own body was full of pairs: pairs of arms, pairs of legs, pairs of eyes, pairs of ears, and paired subsets of two hands: two thumbs, two pinkies, etc. There were pairs everywhere! The idea of pairs must soon have been followed by the idea of duplication: a pair of pairs, two pairs of fingers on each hand, a foursome, and the idea of non-twoness: a pair plus an odd member, a man and mate plus her sister (or two sisters plus a brother).

Along with the idea of pairing must have come the idea of a half. Dividing a fish or some other possession between two people, equally, must have given rise to the concept of a half; the remnants of this experience remain in our language to this day. We speak of one-third, or one-fourth and so on but we never speak of one-second, we speak of a half or of a semi. A semi circle comes from a different source than a third of a circle or a fourth, (where did that quarter-circle come from, perhaps from a half of a half?). Buried deep in many of our ancient languages, "moitie" or "un demi" in French for example, is the concept of a half.

There seems to be no reliable record that helps us understand how or when the leap from two to three and the *discovery* of subsequent numbers and their progression took place. (Did a cosmic hand give the original discoverer a nudge?). To be sure, there is evidence that there was a consciousness of threeness in ancient Egyptian and Chinese records, and also in remnants which survive even today, in the three German language genders for example, but these artifacts are undoubtedly young compared to the age of the discovery itself.

As man evolved he saw that in addition to the presence of pairs, of twoness, there was a commonness among the quantities he could tally by the beans that went beyond twoness: five fingers, five toes, five axes, three birds and two fishes; all these had a common fiveness about them and could be represented by five beans, any five beans, or perhaps one pebble that represented five beans. Some quantities undoubtedly appeared with a greater frequency than others, certainly twos were frequent, and threes and fives. Our ancestor needed names for these frequent quantities. With a giant intellectual leap he recognized the need for names for *any* quantity and number-words were born. This was a great leap forward, an enormous leap, for without it there would be no mathematics! Was this leap inevitable or was there a benign presence inspiring the man who made the discovery?

Once there was the concept of numbers it became necessary to establish a number system. A system of numbers requires a base; in our modern world, and throughout the world, the base is ten; it is the only universal language on the planet! All our numbers involve the first ten single digits and multiples of ten. The base need not be ten, it may be two, twenty, sixty or any other number. Our ancestors in different societies used many different bases.

We are inclined to think only of a number system based on our ten fingers. We forget that some of our ancestors, counting beyond ten, were inclined to take off their shoes. Yet today, when the French get past 79, off come the shoes and we have for 80, "quatre vingt", four twenties. The

French, being French of course, even mix in a little sixty-base, "soixante-dix", sixty-ten for 70. Some primitive societies based their numbers on four because the hand has just four fingers (the thumb is not a finger). There were many choices.

When the bartender asks us today, "How many beers?" we may hold up three fingers, or six, a one-to-one correspondence understood by all, instead of shouting a number. Undoubtedly, that was popular with primitive man, too, and accounts for the popular number systems based on fingers, of which most of us have ten.

But not all fingers are the same. If you wish to signal for one beer do you hold up a thumb? Never, or almost never. (Some say it has been done in Australia!). It is always the index finger. Signal three, the thumb and pinkie disappear leaving the index, middle and ring finger exposed. Signal four, does the thumb appear? Never, even in Australia! So in choosing a numbering system based on his hand man had many choices to consider, and indeed many have appeared among the different ethnic groups.

Ancient societies were isolated; people lived in small groups that became villages. Villages first developed along rivers whose banks provided the environment to grow crops, store excess quantities of grain, and reduce the uncertainties that plagued man when he was only a hunter-gatherer. The rivers that attracted the Neolithic people were the great rivers of Africa, Asia and the Middle East: the Nile, the Tigris and the Euphrates, the Ganges, the Yangtse and the Yellow.

As the number of villages increased, and as the science of farming developed, it became necessary to manage the flow of water. Irrigation, reservoirs, flood control and the control of arable land required cooperative effort among the residents and the creation of an administrative structure that became the foundation of a ruling class. As the societies evolved under the impetus of agriculture they became structured: rulers, soldiers, priests, workers, serfs and slaves. There was enough leisure among the wealthy and the priesthood to study the world about them, to take an interest in pottery decoration and other art and to develop mathematical tools. The engineering of buildings, dams, irrigation systems and the surveying of land areas stimulated the development of mathematics. Dealing with land parcels and bodies of water required a knowledge of measurement and geometry; navigation called for angular directions, distances, and depth measurements; trading among the villages and with caravans from distant sources called for knowledge of arithmetic.

Piles of five beans, of ten nuts, of twenty knots on a string were a first refinement of tallying followed by words that were invented to express these quantities. Number words are not numerals; number words are "one, two, three, eight thousand four hundred twenty-six", and become inconvenient as soon as some sort of record is needed to provide them with permanence. Symbols were the solution to this problem. Dots or slash-marks indicated single items or units, hand-symbols or shell-symbols for five, a man for twenty and so on. These crude symbols provided an improvement over the awkward number words and were subsequently stylized and represented pictorially. Ancient numerical records show us birds and beetles as well as curious symbols at whose derivation we may only guess. The subsequent application of shorthand versions of these pictures led to more sophisticated symbols until the Roman characters: I,V,C,X,L,…and the Indian numerals 1,2,3…we use today evolved.

The evolution from pictorial symbols to more sophisticated characters led ultimately to the *discovery* of abstract numbers as we use them today. These abstract words and symbols may stand for the quantities of any similar or mixed group of items, but they need not stand for anything, they are just **Numbers**!. Imagine the thrill when the first human recognized the significance of this discovery! Numbers may well be the first time that an abstract concept was recognized by Homo sapiens. What a concept! Now there was a common way to deal with different *sets* that had the same number of members: a set of five men, five women or five people, a set of five arrows, a set of 20 trees, a set of 20 tribesmen, or the set of odd numbers or the set of prime numbers!

What a milestone, it was an intellectual leap whose sophistication must have astounded the more astute of our forbears!

Then the discovery of sets of sets; 10 sets of ten, a hundred; ten sets of hundreds; a thousand. These concepts led to the number-words organized in such a way that there was no intellectual limit to the quantity of things which could be counted. We use "illions": millions, trillions, quadrillions, even a word-number for the almost-infinite, "zillions".

Now, lest the reader think that we are dealing with primitive concepts, be advised that the most advanced mathematics of the twentieth century deals with *sets* and *countability*; the same subjects that our hairy ancestor dealt with. For today's mathematicians the sets may have members with no upper limit, an *infinity* of members. Counting the members, or recognizing that the members are not countable (in the one-to-one correspondence with a row of pebbles sense), is a problem which has occupied many very powerful mathematical minds.

Sophisticated Language and Writing Appear

Much evolution was needed to provide the noises a human could produce in order to exchange information regarding numerical quantities. Before these abstract identifiers, these number-words, could exit there had to be a relatively sophisticated language; so the centuries which elapsed between tallying and the development of math may well be associated with the late development of a sophisticated language. The ability to calculate was certainly accelerated with the invention of writing and the ability to inscribe symbols on clay tablet or papyrus. With few exceptions, apart from "idiot savants", our human minds and memories are inadequate to keep track of even simple calculations or algorithms (a computational procedure for solving a certain type of math problem or for programming a computer). We need to "write it down" and record subtotals or steps in a procedure as we pursue the answer. Consequently, writing and the discovery of supplementary memory, abacus, clay tablets, or paper, provided an essential tool in advancing computation and mathematical knowledge. Writing was the only permanent supplementary memory available until the invention of punched cards or punched tape propelled the Jacquard loom and IBM into prominence. Now the marvelous magnetic computer memories with their fantastic capacities enable computation that no amount of paper would ever equal. What a leap from the clay tablet!

Never-the-less, writing is not an essential part of a sophisticated society! The Incas of the Andes region of South America were able to communicate and calculate with the aid of "quipos"; a system in which knotted cords of different colors were suspended from a main cord. The colors identified different items, green for horses, red for men, and the position of the cords on the main cord, the clustering and spacing of the knots and the location and configuration of supplementary cords provided a complete statistical description to a scribe skilled in the art of quipo-reading.

Until this point in our journey we have been describing the world of our ignorant ancestors; ignorant of our world of writing, of science, of mathematics, but very knowledgeable of the forests, the animals, the winds—of nature. These ancestors were by no means stupid, and, as we shall see, they were able to discover many wonders and to invent others. We shall meet them on our journey and marvel at their accomplishments, at their marvelous intellects, at their determination and dedication.

Chapter Four

The Development of Analysis
and Reason

When did the intellectual development of Homo sapiens begin? Of course, it was a gradual process extending throughout Homo sapien's history, but let us choose the beginning of intellectual development to be fifty thousand years ago; the time at which an explosion of progress began. Our predecessors at that time, not so long ago, must have differed but little from the animals that surrounded them. Perhaps there were glimmers of respect for death in crude ceremonies accompanying the burial of the dead, but there was almost assuredly little respect for life in their savage world. They were not animals, but they were not far from it. Here we are, a mere fifty thousand years (2500 generations) later, exploring nearby space, exploring the universe with our telescopes, masters of the atom, unraveling the genetic threads of DNA; awash in new science and knowledge and thinking of ourselves as very sophisticated creatures indeed. How did this amazing metamorphosis come about?

In the forty thousand years that followed the spark which initiated rapid intellectual development Homo sapiens made dramatic progress. But the world in which man lived at the end of that period, only 10,000 years ago, while much advanced from the quasi-animal world of which we have just spoken, was still a very primitive place. The world was full of devils, gods, mysterious events, natural disasters and unexplained phenomena: thunder claps, rainbows, lightning flashes, the darkening of the moon or sun, sudden silence of birds and animals as the eclipses progressed and the motion of sun, moon and stars as they spun round in the heavens. People were consumed by fear; they were full of dread for the unpredictable future. How do the people who lived in that world differ from us? They differ very little in their physical and mental capacity, but there is a vast gulf in terms of the store of knowledge about the world we inhabit. Because we posses that store of knowledge we are men and women of reason; we believe in Causality. For every effect, we believe, there is a cause; we have little fear of the future because we can predict much of it. Our ancestors were ignorant of the physical forces at work on our planet so they invented causes for what they saw and experienced around themselves. The sun was a god who chose to appear in the morning and disappear in the evening; the stars were lights carried in the heavens by mysterious creatures; natural disasters were visited upon humans because of their misbehavior and so on.

The development of reason progressed in unison with man's understanding of his physical world, and his understanding of the physical world progressed in unison with the development of mathematical tools. The superstitions, goblins and monsters, the plethora of gods and devils, the rites of passage and so on disappeared at the same rate that man replaced them with factual knowledge; knowledge of the origin of eclipses, tempests and the terrible natural disasters that have always been man's lot, knowledge of the seasons, the ocean currents, the motion of the planets and the origin of and cures for diseases. Man's knowledge of his physical world and his ability to control that world depended on his ability to analyze and predict events correctly, reliably and quantitatively. **That ability depended on mathematical tools and procedures.** In this way, as this process of intellectual development and the acquisition of physical and mathematical knowledge proceeded, reason supplanted dogma and knowledge supplanted ignorance.

The array of mathematical concepts and procedures enjoyed by our society today is far too vast to attempt to consider in this book. However, in order to understand something of the progress toward enlightenment and the demise of superstition, which were paced by the discoveries of mathematics, we shall take a look at some of the basic math that played an important part in that evolution.

The Role of Mathematics

The history of math is a history of the *discovery* of new worlds, not discovery in a physical/geographical sense (Columbus was a sailor not a mathematician), but rather discovery within a purely intellectual universe of a unique kind; truly, there is no other universe like it. Math is like a stairway, one step leads to the next, one mathematical discovery leads to another. A famous and prolific mathematician of the early 19th century named Carl Gustav Jacob Jacobi said, "The sole end of science is the honor of the human mind, and from this point of view a question concerning number is as important as a question concerning the system of the world".

Mathematics has been the key to analyzing our world and designing the instruments that enable that analysis. Indeed, without mathematical tools progress would cease. Mathematics cooperates with the physical sciences: astronomy, physics, chemistry, biotech, etc., so that we may understand the world about us and ourselves as well. It is the physical sciences which explain to us the way the world is. The physical sciences tool box contains instruments of observation and measurement, mathematical tools, and theories which are intended to predict the results of similar observations in the future. If they are to be useful, those theories must predict future observations in quantitative terms, in numbers. The ability of the United States space program to successfully visit the moon was the result of being able to calculate the orbital trajectories of the spacecraft as they would travel to and from the moon. These calculations were done in advance of the lunar flight. Quantitative predictions depend on mathematical tools. Mathematical tools are the keys to the physical sciences toolbox.

The basic mathematics which enable the study of the world about us are the numbers, geometry, analytic geometry, the calculus and combinatorial analysis. We will take a brief look at these mathematical tools, but we won't have to learn how to use them! The tools may have an unfamiliar and sophisticated appearance and some of the terrain ahead may be a little rough and rocky, but across this intimidating wilderness lies an oasis of knowledge. Courage, gentle reader, let's plow ahead!

As we will speculate, mathematics in cooperation with the physical sciences may unlock doors to understanding more about our role in the universe and may lead us to some glimpses of what may lie beyond the veil that conceals our raison d'être and our destination as the human race.

Those who spent their lives in pursuit of mathematical knowledge seem to have been spurred by two forces: first, the need for tools to solve practical problems and to understand and quantify the forces at work in nature; second, an intellectual drive that was independent of any practical motivation. Throughout history mathematicians have experienced an irresistible drive to explore the properties of numbers and, later, the properties of the calculus, sets, topology etc. for their own sake, a purely intellectual endeavor. There is a remarkable interplay between these two thrusts; the practical problems illuminated the need for pursuit of more sophisticated mathematical properties and the exploration of math for math's sake developed tools that suddenly become useful for solving practical problems. But undoubtedly the initial motivator was to understand the way in which nature worked.

There is a harmony in nature, the Creator's gift, that finds a unique expression in the mathematical equations that permit us to analyze physical phenomena and predict their behavior successfully. That harmony gives us insights into the Creator's nature. It is a fact that many seemingly unrelated natural phenomena are described by the same mathematical equations; that fact is very mysterious and thought-provoking. The motion of the planets obeys the same laws as a ball rolling downhill; the equations which describe the motion of a vibrating violin string are very similar to those that describe the flow of light, and there are many others. Is this harmony just an accident, a coincidence? And, if not, from whence does this harmony originate? Why does it seem that there is a program aimed at making the laws of nature understandable to us Homo sapiens? Furthermore, there are mysteries in the mathematics supporting these equations and especially in the properties exhibited by the numbers that we use so casually every day; mysteries that should make us ask, "Are there clues here that we should be pursuing? Are there keys with which we can begin to unlock the doors which separate us from important answers?".

Mathematical Beginnings

Mathematics is first: searching for the properties of numbers and second: the manipulation of numbers and symbols. How did tallying and counting lead first to arithmetic and then to all of mathematics? History seems to be silent on this subject, so we will indulge in some speculation.

How did Homo sapiens arrive at the elements of arithmetic (which Webster defines as, "the science of computing with positive real numbers")? As he manipulated his rows of beans and pebbles it seems very likely that he soon recognized that two two's and one four were the same quantity. Likewise five pebbles in one pile was the same as a pile of three to which two pebbles had been added. Addition must have been the first element of arithmetical computation to be recognized. Since multiplication is no more than repeated addition he must have soon recognized that two fours were the same as eight and eight was the same as four twos. Soon he has committed to memory a primitive multiplication table. It may have been a very limited table but the *concept* of multiplication had been established. Subtraction must have had its origin in much the same way. Remove two pebbles from a row of four and the remainder pebble count is two. Soon our primitive ancestor must have reconciled the removal of pebbles with the quantity remaining after the removal.

The word division is an arithmetical term but it is more than that. Division implies separating a whole into multiple pieces. In his primitive society Homo sapiens must have faced the problem of division of the spoils of the hunt as a very practical and potentially fatal problem! Dividing a whole among two, four or eight fellows was readily accomplished by progressive halving, but what procedure does one follow if the head count is six? This calls for one halving and then two sharings among three! No doubt the strongest of the three diners had first choice! It seems likely that experience led to the concept of division as the inverse of multiplication, but this last element of arithmetic must have been the most difficult concept to grasp.

Arithmetic was undoubtedly the beginning of mathematical inquiry, but, simple as it may seem to those of us who use it every day, it is not simple and is still a subject for study by the most sophisticated modern mathematicians. Carl Friedrich Gauss, a very sophisticated mathematician who has few peers in the history of mathematics, said in the early 19th century, "Mathematics is the queen of the sciences and arithmetic the queen of mathematics".

The situations which led to arithmetic operations must have led subsequently to the concept of the "unknown quantity". Our ancestor must have asked, "What number is the sum of 17 beans and 32 beans"? At first he probably counted out the two quantities separately, joined them into one pile and then counted the joint quantity. But the concept of assigning an unknown to the total was the beginning of algebra and the manipulation of unknowns and symbols.

It appears that mathematics, the use of numbers and other symbols in the analysis of the world about us, first developed in the area associated with the Tigris and Euphrates rivers in what is now Iraq. The earliest mathematical records are from the Sumerians who were subsequently assimilated by the Babylonians. Both the Babylonians and Sumerians made significant contributions to math, but the Sumerians' math preceded the Babylonians'.

The Sumerians were beginning to develop computational skills as the sun set on the Stone Age, about 8,000 BC. There is some evidence that counting devices (the abacus) were known to these people and they may have had a primitive metrology (the science of weights and measures) used in conjunction with their computational abilities to lay out buildings. And, no doubt at all, some wise administrator invented taxes! Where would we be today without his noble contribution to our culture? Taxes require computation and were undoubtedly a spur to applied mathematics. But the organization of knowledge into what we now call mathematics had to await the development of a written language and the ability to record this knowledge on clay tablets. When baked, these tablets are very rugged and will survive much mishandling and mistreatment. There is a relatively voluminous collection of Sumerian and Babylonian clay tablets. It is not clear to what degree those which have reached us today were baked intentionally or baked by unintentional fires. The Egyptians recorded on papyrus and the Chinese on bamboo, materials which come to us much degraded. Few of the Chinese ancient mathematical records have survived. Most of what we know of the early Egyptians comes to us on only two papyri, the most famous of which is the Papyrus Rhind which dates from the middle of the seventeenth century BC.

The Egyptians appear to have developed mathematical capabilities independently, but there is no way to be sure that they did not receive some mathematical impetus from the Sumerians and Babylonians, their northern neighbors in Mesopotamia; in fact, there is good evidence that such was the case.

A few millennia later, in the triple digit centuries preceding the birth of Christ, mathematical studies were abundant and were flourishing among the Egyptians, Greeks and Arabs in the general area of the eastern Mediterranean. These studies provided the basis for beginning to understand the world about us in a *quantitative* sense, that is to say, to be able to calculate numerical answers to important practical problems: how many bushels of grain will a cylindrical silo of given dimensions hold? Ancient astronomers were be able to predict the occurrence of natural astronomical events (eclipses). But many problems resisted solutions with the mathematical tools available and this led ultimately to the study of mathematics for its own sake.

Geometry

Primitive man had artistic instincts and drives; the famous French cave drawings show beautiful renditions of wild animals. Ancient pottery and basketry show fascinating images of animals as well as intricate geometric designs. The pictorial representation of animals by the cave-artists was an instance of mapping an image of a three dimensional object onto a two dimensional plane; not very different in principle from the bit-mapping that takes place on your computer. The artist needed a concept of space, of line and curve, and of areas. It was probably the artist who established the foundations of geometry. Then, as man evolved into an agrarian society, he developed a need to measure the size of a field and to determine the amount of grain a granary would hold. He needed plane and solid geometry. Geometry must have been a joint development of the artistic and the practical members of ancient societies.

About 2000 BC vast changes were taking place in that part of the ancient world which clustered around the Mediterranean. Iron was replacing bronze. There were many wars. Ancient societies in Egypt and Babylonia were suffering diminished importance as new peoples, the Hebrews, Phoenicians and Greeks, were achieving prominence. An alphabet appeared along with coins; both of these stimulated the economic environment. A merchant class wrested power from the feudal landlords and the towns and cities became trading centers. The Greek self-governing city states arose and, thanks to both brisk and profitable trade and also readily acquired slaves, there was a leisure class with ample time to pursue interests in art, math, music and philosophy.

Geometry germinated and then flowered in ancient Greece. Regrettably, there is little recorded history of the events that marked the very beginning or the motivating factors that sparked interest in this subject. The first Greek figure to appear on the geometrical radar screen is the merchant Thales, of Miletus. He is the (perhaps legendary) father of Greek mathematics. Our knowledge of Thales (ca. 600 BC) and the other men of the early period of the development of geometry in Greece (600-300 BC) comes primarily from a document written by Proclus in the fifth century AD! Yes, 800 years later! Anaxagorous, Hippocrates (no, not that one, this one was a mathematician not a doctor), Eudoxus, Euclid, Eratosthenes, Archimedes, and Pythagorus, of whom we shall hear more later, all appear in Proclus' summary.

Somewhere toward the end of the fourth century BC we first hear of the four divisions into which mathematics was divided: arithmetic, music, geometry and astronomy; these were the liberal arts curriculum of the period. In Greek geometry the emphasis was on derivations and proofs based on rational thinking and logical deduction. The Greeks were convinced that these would lead to the discovery of fundamental principles. There were three problems which were the subject of much study and which were never solved: the trisection of an angle, finding the dimension of the side of a cube twice the volume of a given cube, and finding the area of a square equal to the area of a given circle. None of these can be solved with geometrical techniques.

Euclid, whose book Elements of Geometry is one of the great books of all time, established geometry on a rigorous basis. Euclid and Archimedes, who has been called the greatest mathematician of the ancient world, both lived in the third century BC; so did Apollonius whose investigation of conic sections (circles, ellipses, parabolas and hyperbolas) paved the way for the description of many astronomical phenomena by Kepler and Newton. (Interestingly, the lives of Plato, Archimedes and Alexander the Great, three of the giants of history, shared a part of the same time span).

Archimedes was the first of the three great mathematicians: Archimedes, Newton and Gauss. He lived from 287 to 212 BC. Born into an aristocratic family in Syracuse, Sicily, his father was an astronomer. Archimedes studied for a time in Alexandria, Egypt when he was a young man. He was careless about his dress and ignored his food when he was engrossed in a problem, a characteristic shared by Newton, Gauss, Einstein and other great mathematicians. Everyone knows the story of Archimedes running naked through the streets of Syracuse shouting "Eureka" (I have found it) when he discovered that the weight of a floating body is equal to the weight of the water it displaces. He anticipated both the differential and integral calculus respectively in his studies of the tangent to a spiral and in finding the area included between a parabola and its chord. In addition to his work in mathematics he was a master of applied mechanics; he was familiar with the mysteries of levers and pulleys. He designed magnificent defensive war machines which defeated the Romans' first attack on Syracuse. But the Romans did not give up. They prevailed. Archimedes was killed by a Roman soldier at age 75 during the sack of Syracuse. Of all the mathematicians in human history, Archimedes may have been the greatest. Had Archimedes' math entranced the Greeks instead of Euclid's geometry, the birth of the calculus might have been advanced by 2000 years. This is a very curious fact. Why was there no dominant school following in Archimedes footsteps? Why was Euclid's geometry more important to the Greek scholars than Archimedes' analysis? Was an intermission in man's development necessary for some reason? We must add this to our list of mysteries!

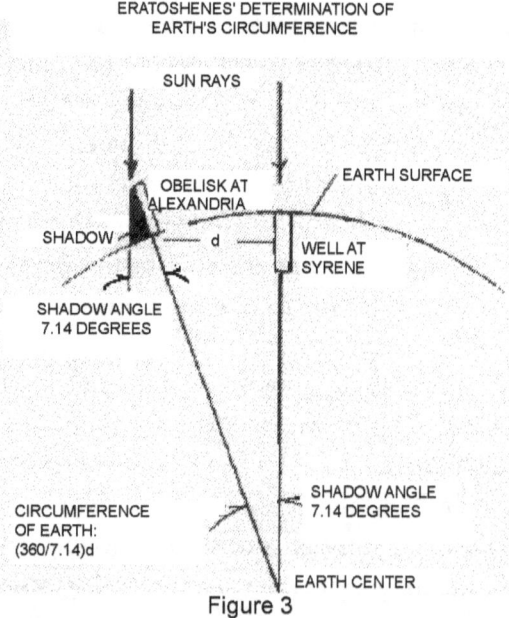

Figure 3

There was, a brilliant Greek geometer named Eratosthenes (276-195 BC) who believed that the earth was a sphere. He made a very remarkable measurement of the circumference of the earth. Figure 3. He heard that the bottom of a well in the town of Syrene was illuminated by the sun at noon, without any shadow, at the time of the summer solstice. He realized that the sun must have been directly overhead. He must also have realized that the earth rotated on a north-south axis. Syrene is directly south of Alexandria. Eratosthenes was also aware that there was always a shadow associated with any object in Alexandria at any time of the year. In order to estimate the circumference of the earth, Eratosthenes measured the length of the shadow of a tall obelisk in Alexandria at the time of the summer solstice. Both the well and the obelisk were perpendicular to the surface of the earth, a sphere. Together with the length of the shadow and the height of the obelisk Eratosthenes determined an angular variation (a variation in latitude) between Syrene and Alexandria of seven degrees and fourteen minutes. After establishing as best he could the distance between Syrene and Alexandria, (there were no available surveys, of course, and distances between cities were estimated in terms of the length of time it took a camel to travel the distance!). Eratosthenes calculated the circumference of the earth to be 28,700 miles. The correct circumference of the earth at the equator is about 24,900 miles. The accuracy of Eratoshenes measurement is astounding!

THE EARTHLY GRID, LATITUDE AND LONGITUDE

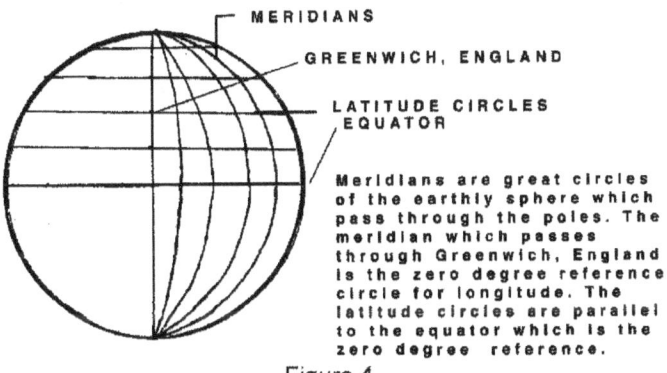

MERIDIANS

GREENWICH, ENGLAND

LATITUDE CIRCLES
EQUATOR

Meridians are great circles of the earthly sphere which pass through the poles. The meridian which passes through Greenwich, England is the zero degree reference circle for longitude. The latitude circles are parallel to the equator which is the zero degree reference.

Figure 4

Another Greek geometer, Hipparchus, (165-127 BC) conceived of meridians, great circles of the earthly sphere passing through the poles. He chose 360 as the number of meridians which would be separated each from its neighbors by one degree (about 70 miles) at the equator. No doubt his choice of a multiple of sixty reflected the influence of a sexagesimal number system. Three hundred sixty degrees mark the circumference of our circles still! Together with circles of latitude the meridians of longitude impose a grid upon the surface of the earth which provides numerical locators for any point on the earth's surface. Figure 4. (We shall have more to say about grids and associated locators when we reach Analytic Geometry).

The discovery of geometry laid the foundation for the elaboration of mathematics beyond the mere manipulation of numbers. Without geometry there would be no analytic geometry, no calculus, and probably very little math beyond arithmetic.

The Importance of Astronomy

Astronomy was of threefold interest to ancient societies: first was the study of the heavens for their own sake, trying to relate heavenly objects and their behavior to man's life on earth; second was to assist the mariners in their journeys across the seas; and the third was to serve the needs of agriculture. Agriculture needed a way to predict the climate, the temperature, the arrival of frosts and snow, the arrival of Spring, the time to harvest and so on. Agriculture needed a calendar. Moon, step forward! What a convenient timekeeper for the ancient calendar-keeper! Not only did the moon's image wax and wane on a 28 day cycle but also the four phases of the moon divided the 28 day period into convenient seven day sub-periods! (Hello there, lucky seven and seven day week). No accident that God made the world in seven days, probably between new moon and first quarter! The solstices, the two times in the year when the sun reaches its maximum excursions north and south of the equator, were well-known to the ancients;

together with the lunar cycle a calendar was available by which ancient man could plan his agriculture.

This interest in the heavens led to their study and the identification of constellations and planets. Ancient mariners must have used the pole-star and the constellations for navigation; they had to make use of angular directions to find their way about the seas, and undoubtedly developed some concepts of the circle and perhaps the sphere. Mariners were familiar with the fact that the tallest part of a distant ship appeared first as the ship approached, and some must have surmised that the ship was traveling on the surface of a sphere. This speculation on the nature of the earth on which we walk remained for Eratosthenes, of whom we have just spoken, to document. Unusual astronomical events such as eclipses of the sun and moon, planetary conjunctions and oppositions, supernovas and the like were noted, and efforts to predict their occurrence stimulated an interest in mathematics. But the results of mathematical calculations were full of sizeable residual errors. Errors in land measurements and area calculations led to disputes. Errors in the pursuit of irrigation and agriculture led to hunger. Reductions in the size of the errors was essential; there was a clear need for better estimates and approximations.

Approximations

Mathematicians love approximations because they lead to solutions for problems that have no exact answer. However it was not always so. In ancient days, approximations were hated and despised by a purist elite because there was a grave fear that math would never be an exact science. The ancients, the Greeks in particular, attached great importance to exact solutions; the inability to trisect the angle, to find an exact value for pi (the ratio of the circumference of a circle to its diameter), and the discovery of irrational numbers greatly disturbed the philosophers of the day. Irrational numbers are numbers which can not be expressed as the ratio of two integers i.e. two whole numbers. Pi is such a number, the square root of two is such a number, and roots of algebraic equations may be such numbers also.

Zeno, who lived in the fifth century BC, is famous for his paradoxes. One of these, familiar to many of us, is the traveler who must first travel half way to his destination, then half the remainder, then half of the next remainder etc. Consequently the traveler will never reach his destination! The rigorous math needed to identify the fallacies in this kind of paradox did not yet exist. (Regrettably, the remnants of this kind of thinking are with us yet today.)

Concepts dealing with the infinitely large and the infinitely small, with the size of a point, the width of a line, with orders of the infinitely large and the infinitely small were debated among the wisest men of the pre-Christian era, but there were no rigorous logical processes to lead them to conclusions which could withstand the challenges of their peers. Eudoxus, in the fourth century BC, began to rectify this shortcoming and paved the way for Euclid's axioms (self-evident truths) which have survived to this day as the bane of highschool geometers.

The concept of a circle has been with us for a long time. The discs of the sun and moon, pots made on the potter's wheel, the wheels of chariots, the motion of water in a vortex, the segment of a circle which a rainbow exhibits, all of these and the ceremonial circles of ancient religions and primitive councils called attention to this most fundamental form. As agriculture developed and cylindrical jars and storage bins were used for granaries it became necessary to be able to calculate the volume of these containers. The ancient mathematician knew that the volume of a cylinder equaled the area of the circular base multiplied by the length of the cylinder. But calculating the area of the circular base was another matter! How should he calculate the area of a circle?

Of course we all know the formula today, the area of a circle is pi x radius x radius. But this simple equation involves several important concepts: the concept of a perfect circle, the radius of the circle, and the numerical value of pi. See Figure 5 for the geometrical definition of pi.

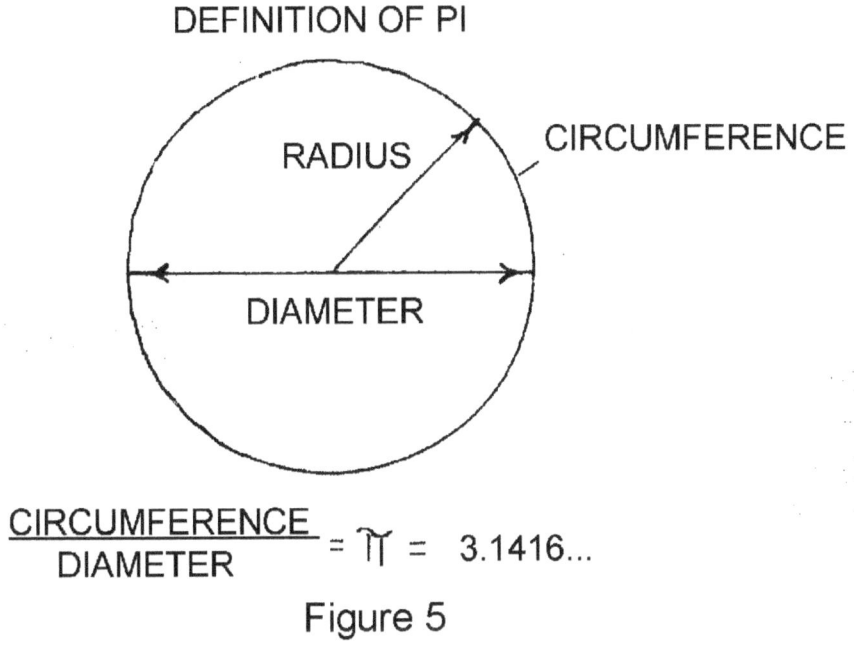

DEFINITION OF PI

RADIUS

CIRCUMFERENCE

DIAMETER

$$\frac{\text{CIRCUMFERENCE}}{\text{DIAMETER}} = \pi = 3.1416...$$

Figure 5

We can choose an exact number for the radius, but we can never calculate the exact value for the area because pi is a decimal number with a never ending sequence of digits: 3.141592653589793...., it goes on forever. We accept this today without much thought, but it drove the ancients bonkers! The world of the intellectuals, the philosophers, the mathematicians of that day, required exact answers, and those exact answers were not forthcoming! They believed that the ratio of the circumference of a circle to its diameter **must** be able to be expressed as the ratio of two integers. They refused to accept an inexact, approximate, answer. The accountants of that time used approximations because they needed answers to practical problems, so they found that the ratio of two integers: 22/7=3.142857142857142857...was an approximate value for pi which gave answers that were inexact but very satisfactory for practical purposes.

But the purists were adamant; they would not accept an inexact answer. (Notice the repeating integers in the decimal: 142857; we shall have more to say about this kind of curiosity later).

There is always a residual uncertainty about the area of a circle, the size of the residue depends, of course, on where we choose to truncate the value for pi, that is to say, where we choose to terminate the approximation. We can make the residue as small as we choose, but we can not eliminate it *except "in the limit" as we permit the number of digits in the value of pi to reach infinity.* This concept of limiting processes is the foundation of much of modern mathematics. More about limits later.

The Golden Age of Greece began in the fifth century BC. It was a time of vigorous intellectual activity much of which, perhaps most of which, was mathematical in nature. One of the problems which occupied the philosophers was the "quadrature of the circle", that is to say, find a geometrical square whose area is exactly equal to the area of a given geometrical circle. In order to solve this problem an exact value for pi was essential. Of course, no one knew at that time that there was no exact value. In an effort to find this elusive number some very clever techniques were employed; one of these was to inscribe the circle in a many sided polygon and then inscribe another many sided polygon within the circle. Figure 6.

THE EXHAUSTION METHOD OF EUDOXUS

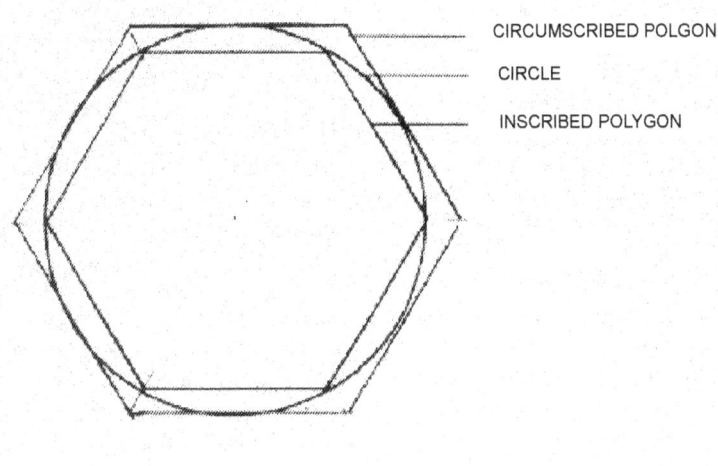

CIRCUMSCRIBED POLGON

CIRCLE

INSCRIBED POLYGON

Figure 6

As the number of sides increased (of course, the areas of the polygons could be determined exactly) there were two numbers, one greater than the circular area and one less, but both converging on the number which was the area of the circle. Alas, the two numbers never converged on a single finite value. The Greeks were using the polygons to approximate the area of the circle. As they increased the number of sides of the polygon they were using the beginning of a limiting process, a profound mathematical discovery for which conceptual clarity and a rigorous definition lay hundreds of years in the future.

During the Golden Age of Greece the Greeks were well on their way to initiating the development of the whole body of mathematics and science. Euclid laid the foundations of geometry; Archimedes had his hands around tangents and limiting processes; Pythagorous studied the properties of numbers and was the first experimentalist as well. In the third century BC Appolonius explored the fringes of Analytic

Geometry and Aristarchus proposed a heliocentric model for the sun and its planets. The Roman Empire had not yet conquered the Ancient World. Why was this promising beginning nipped in the bud? Why did learning atrophy in the last few centuries BC? The history of learning since the beginning of the thirteenth century has been one of exponential growth! Based on recent experience, we should have to say that learning is continuous, nothing will interrupt it. **Why was that not the case in Greece during the last few centuries before Christ? Did some cosmic foot apply the brakes?**

Chapter Five

Numbers

A quote from Al-Khwarizmi circa the ninth century AD, "When I considered what people generally want in calculating, I found that it is always a number".

Say to someone, "I want to play a little mathematical game with you and, to begin, I want you to write down your age." Hand them a pad and pencil. Will they write "twenty-six"? Never, or, almost never. They will write 26. Why? Why a symbol instead of a word? Surely, in the history of man, the words must have come first and the symbols later, as a kind of shorthand. In fact, the symbols seem to be essential. How would one ever cope with a corporate balance sheet if all the numerals were words? In what follows we shall use the "English" version of number words and number symbols, although these number symbols are really adopted from the Indian/Arabic.

The number symbols we use every day are used every day by every country on the face of this planet! It is a universal language of numbers, the only universal language with which we Homo sapiens communicate. Why is this so? No doubt it is the efficiency of the decimal system. Ancient societies used the letters of the alphabet to indicate numeric values; the Greek alphabet was used in that way and mathematicians still use Greek letters for variable quantities; why not for numbers? Too cumbersome!

The decimal system contains a large variety of numbers: positive, negative, real and imaginary numbers; rational, irrational, prime and complex numbers. Furthermore, it contains many curiosities and mysteries. We shall take a limited look at this fascinating subject.

The Natural Numbers and Zero

Somewhere, sometime in the past, the concept of the "natural numbers" 1,2,3,4,5,…was *discovered*. These are, of course, all the numbers which can be put into a one-to-one correspondence with a row of beans; this is the natural thing to do, e.g. they are called the natural numbers! The natural numbers are extremely important to modern mathematicians for the same kind of reason that they were important to our ancestor; modern mathematicians test sets, often infinite sets, of numbers for their properties by determining if the members of the sets can be put into a one-to-one correspondence with the natural numbers.

At first there was no zero. How does one have a bean to represent no item at all? At first, in some cultures, it was represented by a gap, in others by a special symbol. All the other numbers can be put into a one to one correspondence with a quantity of beans, but not zero! In the Indian numerals we use today zero can be nothing or it can be a multiplier: $0+4=4$, 4+nothing is 4, but 40 is ten times 4 and 400 one hundred times 4! How can this be, one number with two values! At other times, as a multiplier, it erases a number, $(4\times0=0)$, or it can drive it to infinity $(4/0=\text{infinity})$. At other times it behaves not like a multiplier, but like nothing at all, as if it weren't there: $04=4$. And any number raised to the zeroth power equals one! These strange and mysterious properties of zero were very disconcerting to mathematicians of the thirteenth and fourteenth centuries. Was zero a number? If not, what was it? As late as the fifteenth century its nature was still being debated in spite of the fact that Fibonacci seems to have had it right in the thirteenth century. The concept of zero is a difficult concept and no doubt the *discovery* of zero came many decades, more probably many centuries, after the discovery of the natural numbers. Some believe the evidence shows its origin to be in China. Wherever its origin it is a most remarkable entity. Zero has many of the properties of other numbers and yet it has many properties that other numbers do not have; it is truly unique. *Why?* Why is zero, the least of numbers, the most unusual? Who decided that it was to be that way?

Most mathematicians now include zero with the natural numbers although for some time the purists referred to "the natural numbers and zero"; we will include it, so henceforth the **Natural Numbers** are 0,1,2,3,4,5,…i.e. all the **Positive Integers and Zero.**

Certain numbers came to have greater significance to ancient societies than others. Cults developed which attributed mystery and religious significance to certain numbers. One of the most famous of these cults was founded by a man named Pythagorus who lived in the sixth century BC in Greece.

Pythagorous

Pythagorus is a giant in the history of man's discoveries about the natural world for he is believed to be the father of experimental science. The birth of experimentation is an enormously important event, for it was the first time that man had interjected himself into natural phenomena to attempt to ascertain the cause of certain effects. Before Pythagorus man was only an observer of whatever happened around him, he made no effort to set up an experiment and draw conclusions from his experimental results. Pythagorus was interested in music, and, in particular, in musical notes. He fashioned a crude but elegant experiment which disclosed that the ratio of a note, its octave, its fifth and its fourth were in the ratio of 2:1; 3:2; and 4:3. He was so taken with this fact that he adopted a creed that "All is number", number was the beginning, the be-all, and the end-all of the universe. Nothing illustrated this fact more clearly than the beautiful musical harmonies! The principles of mathematics were the principles of everything!

Alas, instead of pursuing his experimental triumph he turned to numerology, mystical religion, and the leadership of a cult which worshiped numbers. Experimental science lay dormant for many centuries until it was resurrected by Galileo. Galileo is known as the founder of experimental physics, and he deserves the title, but Pythagorous really opened the door.

Why was there this enormous quiescent period in the pursuit of experimentation, and what awakened it in the 17th century? Is this anomaly just an aberration or was there some *reason* why experimentation should remain dormant for more than a thousand years? Why does it appear that the scenario was rewritten? Who rewrote it? *Might we suspect intervention?*

In the not so primitive period several hundred years BC (not so long ago, really) secret societies, of which the Pythagoreans are the prime example, guarded mathematical knowledge and are said to have murdered those who shared the knowledge with non-members. What kind of knowledge did they guard so diligently? Much was inferential in nature, they endowed a few curious properties of numbers with unwarranted importance. From these meager beginnings they developed an extremely complex numerology. The launching pad for their beliefs is the fact that the sum of the first four numerical digits is ten: $1+2+3+4=10$. Four had great significance because earth, water, fire and air were the constituents of the universe. Ten had great significance because it was the sum of the first four numbers and also, since ten was the basis for their number system, all subsequent numbers were obtained by adding the single digits to multiples of ten. Odd numbers were male, even numbers female! Some numbers had geometric attributes: triangular numbers: $1,3,6,10,....$, numbers which can be represented by a vertical assembly of dots in the form of a triangle (for ten, four dots on the bottom, three in the next layer, two on the next and one on top, just like your bowling alley) and square numbers: 1,4,9,16,...., (where for sixteen for example, four rows of four dots one above the other, form a square) carried mystical significance to the Pythagoreans. These examples merely scratch the surface of an elaborate numerology to which members of the Pythagorean Brotherhood devoted their lives. Numerology has been popular for thousands of years and has been embraced by men of great intelligence. Johann Kepler, who discovered the three laws of planetary orbits and thereby paved the way for Newton to discover the laws of gravitation, was deep into numerology, and this interest led him to his search for numerical relationships in the planetary orbits. Fortunately for us, he found them!

Before we leave Pythagorus to his ascetic contemplation of numbers, we must mention that Pythagorus was a guest in Milo's house for more than twenty years. Milo was the strongest man, the best athlete, and the richest man in the Greek town of Croton. Pythagorous' interest in numbers did not blind him to Theano, the beautiful and intelligent daughter of Milo. He married Theano who was several decades younger than he; she bore him several children and was undoubtedly a great comfort to him in his old age!

Remember the Pythagorean Theorem that you were taught in high school?

The square **on** the hypotenuse of a right triangle is equal to the sum of the squares **on** the other two sides.

A right triangle is one which has one right angle (90 degree angle). (Two intersecting straight lines which are perpendicular to each other form four right angles).

See Figure 7 for the geometric interpretation of this statement that the Greeks were taught.

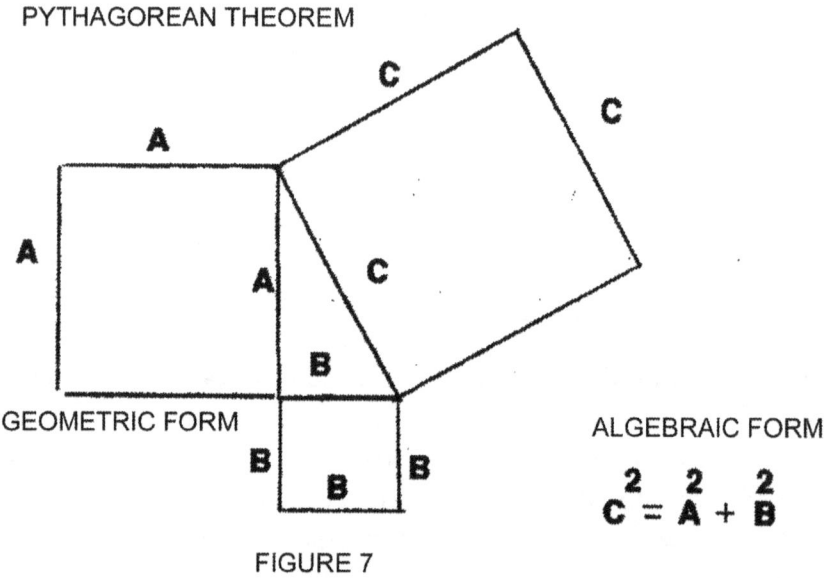

PYTHAGOREAN THEOREM

GEOMETRIC FORM

ALGEBRAIC FORM

$$C^2 = A^2 + B^2$$

FIGURE 7

A geometrical square is constructed on the hypotenuse of the right triangle (the longest side is the "hypotenuse"). The hypotenuse forms one side of the square and the three other sides are the same length as the hypotenuse. Then squares are constructed on the other two sides of the triangle in the same manner. It can be proven using the rules of plane geometry (that you learned in high school) that the area of the square drawn on the hypotenuse equals the sum of the areas of the squares drawn on the other two sides. The Greeks knew almost no algebra, their mathematics was accomplished with compass and straight edge ruler by drawing figures on a piece of paper and making logical deductions following the rules of geometry.

The Pythagorean Theorem is often taught as an algebraic equation: "The square *of* the hypotenuse is equal to the sum of the squares *of* the other two sides" i.e. $a^2 + b^2 = c^2$. By a^2 we mean (a)x(a); by b^2 we mean (b)x(b), etc. The 'exponent', two in these cases, is said to square the quantity of which it is the exponent since (a)x(a) is the area of a square with sides equal to a. See Fig. 7. (If the exponent were three the quantity would be said to be cubed since (a)x(a)x(a) is the volume of a cube with sides equal to a.) This algebraic formulation of Pythagorus' theorem changes the original Greek geometric concept into an algebraic one and the student thereby misses an important geometric image. The algebraic formula is a convenient one to remember, but it would be all Greek to the Greeks!

The *discovery* of the Pythagorean Theorem led to an enormous amount of mathematical interest and effort in the millenium preceding the birth of Christ; since then, equations of the same form have occupied many prominent mathematicians who were trying to prove Fermat's Last Theorem; more of that fascinating tale later.

There are some right triangles for which the numbers involved in the Pythagorean Theorem are all whole numbers (integers). The triangle whose sides measure 3,4 and 5 units has corresponding squares of 9,16 and 25 (9 + 16 = 25) and is the best known, but 5,12,13 (25+144=169) and 8,15,17 are other "Pythagorean Triples".

These "triples" were known to the ancients in Greece and those in Babylonia and probably other eastern Mediterranean countries. There is also some evidence (and considerable questioning debate) that the residents of England, about 2000 BC, also knew them. They were thought to have mystical properties; they were important in establishing the dimensions of religious altars in the eastern Mediterranean as well as religious structures such as Stonehenge in far away England. Mathematics, numbers, were important to these ancient societies not only for solving practical problems but also for constructing temples, altars and other buildings. Numbers had both mystical and religious significance.

Modern Mystery Numbers

The same is true for us today, we have some numbers that are more "important" than others. Seven seems to be the most important of all: seven days for Creation, seven seals of Revelations, seven plagues, seven days in the week, lucky seven, seven stars in the Dipper, seven branches in the menorah, the seventh son of a seventh son, and many more. There are 28 days in the lunar and menstrual cycles; these may well be related to the importance of the number seven, for the four phases of the lunar cycle (new moon, half moon, full moon, half moon, new moon) create a base of seven days. Primitive man lived close to the sun, moon and stars, and attributed mystical properties to them, and doubtless to any numbers which could be associated with their behavior. There are seven prominent heavenly bodies visible to the naked eye: sun, moon, Venus, Mars, Jupiter, Saturn, Mercury. They were given great significance in ancient religions, their names abound in Greek mythology. Some scholars believe the origin of the seven-day week can be attributed to these heavenly bodies. There is no doubt about the names for the days of the week beginning with *Sun*day. Is this the source of the respect shown for number seven? Or is seven related to the seven bodily orifices? We have two ear holes, two nostrils, a mouth and two more the reader can identify. Whence the origin of the universal regard for 7?

Why is "three" (the Trinity) so important in Christianity, some other religions and elsewhere? It echoes from the past in languages that recognize male, female and neuter. The number three is of enormous importance because it is the departure from the "I-Everything Else" dichotomy. No doubt it was nascent in the "I-you-everything else" world of our hairy ancestor. Beyond three is the whole sequence of numbers, and without doubt that accounts for its early religious significance and the hangover lasting to this day. Why is twelve accorded great stature among the numbers: apostles, the clock face, months in the year, number of jurors? Why are 13 and 666 "sinister/unlucky" numbers? The ancients were superstitious about numbers and accorded them religious significance. Those of our ancestors who possessed the arcane knowledge of numbers were feared and accorded superior rank in primitive societies. Even today those who possess critical number information (the Federal Reserve Chairman) have great power and associated mystique!

Some Curious Properties of Numbers

Let us pause for a moment and think about what numbers really are. Take a large coffee sack from Brazil and spread the multitude of coffee beans out in a straight line. Then ask yourself, "How shall I bestow a separate identifier on each coffee bean and be able to reconstruct their sequence if they become mixed up?" The solution is to number the coffee beans. That is all that numbers are, basically, a way to keep track of items. But man has discovered that these numbers can be manipulated by addition, subtraction, multiplication and division which gives him supplementary useful information: totals, differences, products and ratios. He has also discovered, as we shall see, that these bean-identifiers have some very strange properties. Why? It makes no sense! These numbers are only a different manifestation of a row of beans! Many of these strange properties seem to be only curiosities, they seem to have no useful purpose. Why are they there? For the most part the universe we live in makes rational sense; why do not these properties of the numbers? Who is responsible for math being the way it is? Will some ultimate revelation answer that question? Pythagorous saw mystical religious properties in the numbers. Plato believed that the Creator was a mathematician. After considering the strange properties we are about to look at, what conclusion do you reach?

Perfect Numbers

Somewhere along the line someone *discovered* "perfect numbers"; numbers which equal the sum of their factors. By a "factor" we mean an integer which, when divided into the number of which it is a factor, yields an integer as the result.

For example, one and two are factors of four, three is not. The number six is the product of its factors: 1,2 and 3. 6 = 1x2x3 and is also equal to the sum of these factors, 6=1+2+3. Likewise 28 = 1+2+4+7+14 is the sum of its factors; how many more can you identify? (The next one is about 468 numbers ahead of the last). Thanks to a gentleman of the first century AD, Nicomachus by name, here is a method by which these "perfect" numbers can be found. We write down 1 followed by all the powers of two: 1,2,4,8,16,32,….We then add them progressively: 1+2=3 and we stop if we see a prime number as the sum (a prime number has no factors other than one: 3,7,13,17 for example). In our example 3 is a prime; we then multiply the sum by the last number added, in our case 2, and the answer is 6, a perfect number. The next sum is 1+2+4=7, another prime, multiply by 4, the last number added, and the result is 28, a perfect number. And so on, it continues.

Why are all the "perfect" numbers even numbers? *Now this is really odd!* (No pun intended!) Why do all of them end in either six or eight? Why does the procedure for finding them work? It makes no sense that they should be bound to the prime numbers in such an unexpected fashion! Why are they? One is almost certain that there is some sort of a clue buried in here somewhere! What is it?

The Partial Sum of the Odd Numbers

There is another partial sum that conceals startling consequences.

Take the sum of two or more numbers in the sequence of odd numbers beginning with one:1+3+5+7+..., each "partial" sum is the square of the number of numbers in the sum. Sum the first two numbers: 1+3=4. There are two numbers in the sum and the square of two, i.e.2x2, is 4. Sum the first three numbers in the sequence: 1+3+5=9, there are three numbers in the sum and 3x3=9; 1+3+5+7+9+11=36, six numbers in the sum and 6x6=36, etc. Is this not a bit strange? Is it not a bit mysterious? These are just bean numbers after all, would one expect them to have any curious properties at all? Is someone trying to tell us something?

Repeating Decimals

Do you remember how to do long division? Let's divide 1 by 1+x where we restrict x to lie between zero and one. See Fig.8.

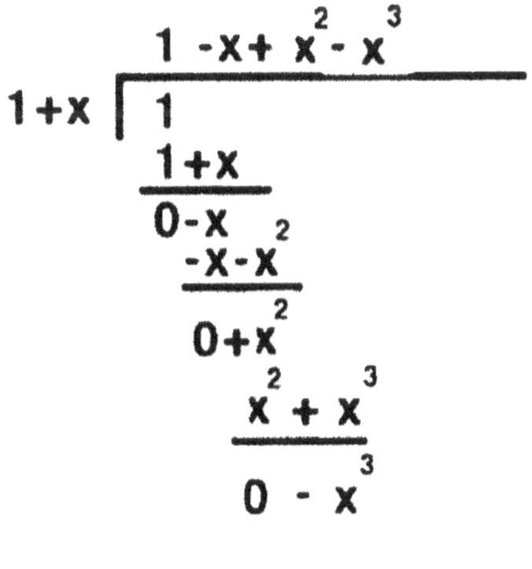

$$
\begin{array}{r}
1 - x + x^2 - x^3 \\
1+x \overline{\smash{\big)}\ 1} \\
\underline{1+x} \\
0 - x \\
\underline{-x - x^2} \\
0 + x^2 \\
\underline{x^2 + x^3} \\
0 - x^3
\end{array}
$$

FIGURE 8

We have developed an infinite series for $1/(1+x)=1-x+x^2-x^3+...$ This series never ends but we can get an excellent approximate answer by adding several terms.

Let's see what 1/1.01 equals and compare it with the first few terms of the series. $1/1.01=0.99009900990099009900...$ Adding the first four terms of the series $(1-.01+.0001-.000001)$ gives us 0.990099, correct to six digits. As you can see, for small values of x the series **converges** toward the exact number very rapidly. (It converges to a correct answer only for $0<x<1$; read that x greater than zero and less than one). There is another interesting thing in this little exercise, notice that the 9900 figures in the quotient repeat forever; these repeating figures are typical of the repeating figures that will appear in the decimal quotient of two rational numbers (two whole numbers) when the quotient does not terminate. For example, $1/2=0.5$ terminates, it is exact, but:

$1/3=0.333333333333...$ repeats without end.

$15/13=1.153846153846153846...$ has six digits which repeat endlessly.

This is very curious, it's as if something was planted there for us to *discover* and wonder about; and to realize that this mathematical curiosity will be the same for all other occupants of the galaxy. Something that can be contemplated only in our minds, intellectually, because there is nothing physical to relate this to. If indeed something of an intellectual stimulus was planted there for us to find what were the planter's intentions? Did he want to make our lives more interesting and to encourage us to pursue intellectual pursuits because of the esoteric rewards? Why do the quotients of rational numbers exhibit this odd behavior?

Fibonacci's Sequence and The Golden Ratio

Enter a man of the thirteenth century, Leonardo Pissarro, better known to us today as Fibonacci. He traveled widely in the Near East and Asia, and

is believed to be responsible for importing from India the numerical notation that we use today. Fibonacci was a successful merchant and an accomplished mathematician; he studied algebraic problems and probably
applied a method of successive approximations to his studies. He had an
especial interest in numbers; he discovered a sequence of numbers which
bears his name: 0,1,1,2,3,5,8,13,21,34,55.89…. Each number in this
sequence is the sum of the preceding two numbers. As the numbers
become larger and larger the ratio of one of the numbers in the sequence to
the number which precedes it becomes closer and closer to, i.e. converges
toward, 1.61803…. (This number is known as "The Golden Ratio"). For
example 8/5=1.600; 21/13=1.6153846; 89/55=1.6181818…and so on;
the larger the adjacent numbers in the series the more nearly their ratio
approaches the "Golden Ratio". This number, 1.618…, was probably
given its name by the Ancient Greeks; it was known to Euclid. The
astronomer Kepler dubbed it "The Divine Proportion".

Remarkably, Mother Nature seems to know Fibonacci's sequence.
Count the petals in a flower, you are likely to find 3, 5, 8,…; count the
number of stamen or the spiral formations on a leaf and there too you will
probably find a one-to-one correspondence with one of the Fibonacci
numbers. Talk to an artist, he will tell you that these numbers influence
the location of the subjects in his painting. They help him make a choice
which is pleasing to the eye; he will talk about the Golden Ratio. Let's
spend a moment with the artist to learn a little about how he does this.

He will choose his canvas to have dimensions in accordance with the
"Golden Ratio". Perhaps he will choose a canvas 10 feet wide and 6.18
feet high, 10/6.18 = 1.618. Then he will choose a primary "center of interest". It is to this point on the canvas that he hopes to draw your eye. He
will draw a vertical line 6.18 feet from the left side of the ten foot wide
canvas. Then he will draw a horizontal line 3.82 feet (6.18/1.618 = 3.82)
from the top of the canvas. The intersection of these two lines will locate
his "center of interest". He will capture the eye by a combination of location, color and value (luminous intensity, i.e. darkness or lightness). The

two lines he has drawn will mark off smaller rectangles which are also in the Golden Ratio. He will locate secondary points of interest within these rectangles by the same process. The next time you visit an Art Gallery remember the Golden Ratio. You will find that square canvasses tend to jar your eye; you will find others in the Golden Ratio where the artist has employed the procedure we have just outlined and you will find these canvasses very pleasing!

The Golden Ratio was known to the Greeks and Egyptians hundreds of years before Fibonacci. They first arrived at this ratio by finding the Golden Cut. Remember that geometry, and therefore ratios, were almost a religion to the Greeks. To arrive at the Golden Cut they divided a line in such a way that the ratio of the larger portion to the smaller is the same as the ratio of the whole line length to the larger portion. The ratio of each of these two sets of line lengths is the Golden Ratio. See Figure 9.

THE GOLDEN RATIO

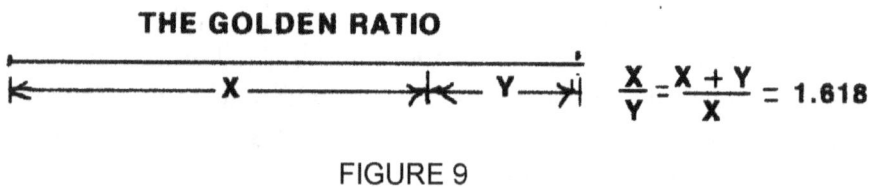

$$\frac{X}{Y} = \frac{X+Y}{X} = 1.618$$

FIGURE 9

Let's put this statement in the form of a simple equation. Choose the total length of the line to be composed of two pieces x and y then the total line length is x+y; choose x larger than y such that the ratio $x/y=(x+y)/x$. Solve the equation for the ratio x/y; you will find that the ratio x/y is 1.618.... Curiously, if we turn the ratio upside down the ratio $y/x = x/(x+y)=0.618$. The inversion of the ratio, which is called the reciprocal, is 0.618…! The ratio and its reciprocal differ by unity, i.e. 1.618 -0.618 = 1. This relationship is unique among all the numbers! Why does this unique relationship apply to the Golden Ratio which nature embraces with such enthusiasm? Very thought provoking!

The great Kepler called The Golden Ratio "The Divine Proportion" because it embodies a mystical beauty when expressed in art and architecture. We are reminded of the mystical mathematical beauty Pythagorus found in the harmonies of music. Some of the magnificent buildings of ancient Greece have proportions that are in the Golden Ratio, For some mysterious reasons these proportions are remarkably pleasing to the eye.

But back to the Fibonacci series. Ask a weaver how she chooses the stripes created by her warp threads and you will hear of these numbers again. We respond, we children of Mother Nature, we "resonate" to these numbers as do the flowers. Find a stock market speculator, a "technician"; he will tell you about the utility of this sequence as he pursues his arcane forecasts of future prices.

We are searching for clues to the nature of the Creator. Here we seem to find the same thumbprint in a number of different and unrelated areas. Is this not strange? Might we not suspect that the Creator was particularly entranced with this series of numbers and with the Golden Ratio? Does this not make us suspect some kind of clue may be submerged in these mathematical oddities? How does it happen that we humans, the stock market and many plants resonate to these numbers? They are, after all, only numbers, they only identify certain members of a row of beans. Why do we humans react to their manifestation in geometrical form with emotion? Is it because we sense, rather than see, the presence of the Creator's thumbprint?

Prime Numbers

And then there are the mysterious mystery numbers, the prime numbers; numbers that are divisible to yield an integer quotient only when divided by one and themselves. For example, 29 is a prime number; divide

29 by any number other than 1 and 29 and the quotient will not be an integer (a whole number). Two (the only even prime) three, five, seven, 11, 13, 17, 19 are examples of prime numbers. These strange numbers, which seem to have no real pattern to them, were *discovered* many centuries ago. They play a central and exceptionally important role in mathematics. They are also central to sophisticated cryptography. Is there a supremely sophisticated cryptogram, some transcendently important message, encoded into these numbers or their sequence? Will we someday discover the Prime Code just as we have discovered the DNA code? And what might it tell us?

Why do these numbers, with no apparent rhyme or reason to their appearance in the sequence of all the natural numbers, occupy such an important role in mathematics? Why are the "prime number beans" so special?

Examples of Unusual Properties of Prime Numbers

Let's pause for a moment and explore some of the unusual properties of prime numbers.

As a mathematics professor would say:

"Consider the set of numbers = 4n + 1, where n is a positive integer".

First a definition of the word "set". When it is used in a mathematical context: a "set" is the totality of all numbers which satisfy a given mathematical condition. (Be reminded of a set of dishes which satisfy the condition that they will provide place settings for a table of twelve!). In this example the condition is that each member of the set be a number drawn from the set of numbers = 4n + 1 where "n" can take on any integer value: 1,2,3,4,5,6,.....

For our first example choose n = 1, then 4n + 1 = 4x1 + 1 = 5. So 5 is the first number in the set. The next number in the set appears when n=2. Then 4n+1=4x2+1=9. The first few numbers in this set are 5 (n = 1), 9 (n

=2), 13,(n=3),17,21,25,29,33,37.... and the set continues forever (without limit) each member of the set being 4 units greater than the one before.

Pick any prime number from the set (in the set listed in the previous sentence all the numbers except 9,21, 25 and 33 are primes). You will find, as Fermat did in the seventeenth century, and as he proved, that any prime drawn from this set is the sum of two squares, and only two! Take 29 = 25 + 4, (5x5 + 2x2); 37 = 6x6 + 1x1, etc. Now, is this peculiar or what? It is mysterious, mind boggling, weird; and without explanation!

Prime numbers were known in ancient times. The ninth book of Euclid's 'Elements' contains a proof that the number of primes is infinite. Eratosthenes devised a method for finding primes which is known as "The Sieve of Eratosthenes". In more recent times we use digital computers. In 1996, the largest known prime was:

$2^{1,396,259}$ -1 (Two multiplied by itself 1,396,259 times -1)

This prime number contains 420,921 digits! It is not quite infinite, but it will certainly fill up a sheet of paper.

Let's look at another property of prime numbers; this one will take a bit more thought:

"Consider the set of numbers formed by multiplying any number "n" by itself p times (p is any prime number) and subtracting from this product n."

An example: n = 5; p = 3, nxnxn = 5x5x5 = 125, subtract 5 and this member of the set is 120. Fermat discovered that any member of this set will be divisible (dividend an integer) by the p used to form it. In our example 120/3 = 40, the dividend 40 is an integer, and therefore p = 3 is a factor! p is the **number of times we multiplied, p is not a multiplier!** How can it *always* be a factor? Weird stuff again!

Is there some sort of message in this melange of curious properties? Perhaps the message is simply to be aware of the possibility of messages! Perhaps there *is* a message somewhere and these curious properties are a component of the total message. (Or is it so mind-boggling that we should simply turn away and say, "Oh, why puzzle over these numerical mysteries? Let's abandon the search for understanding!")

Rational and Irrational Numbers

Primitive man had the problem of dealing with portions of a whole; how did one apportion a whole fish among two (or more!) people? At first the problem was probably solved with muscle, and there was no need for numbers, but at some point the need to solve the problem with equity became important. Mathematics, fractions, to the rescue. Fractions! The peril of many a modern student. There are many fascinating disclosures in the literature of the clever but cumbersome way in which the Egyptians, for example, dealt with the problem of fractions, but we will pass right by that swamp and take this opportunity to introduce the subject of **Rational Numbers**. As the name implies, rational numbers are the ratio of two whole numbers, integers, not decimals: 7/64; 32/874; 1/2 are rational numbers. These are also known as fractions, but to the mathematician they are a *set* of importance, and must be included in our system of numbers for completeness: **The Set of Rational Numbers.** Since every natural number is the ratio of that number to one, the set of rational numbers includes all the natural numbers.

Are there numbers which do not belong to the set of rational numbers? Indeed, there are the **Irrational Numbers**. An irrational number is some never-ending decimal number which is not equal to any integer divided by another integer. Some never-ending decimal numbers are rational numbers. For example 4/3=1.3333333333.... but pi = 3.1415926535...is not equal to any ratio of two integers, therefore it is **irrational.** The first irrational numbers discovered are believed to be the square root of two and pi. By the "square root" of a number "n" we mean that number which multiplied by itself produces "n" as the product. Thus the square root of 4 is 2; 2x2=4. The origin of the term comes from a geometrical square. If the side of the square is two the area of the square is four. The Pythagoreans are believed to be the first to discover that the square root of two could not be represented by the ratio of two whole numbers (integers). It presented itself to the Pythagoreans as they pondered the length of the hypotenuse of a right triangle with equal sides of unit length, that is to say that the length of each side is equal to one. (The unit of measure may be one inch, one foot, one mile, but the number associated with the measure is one = unity). The squares of each of the two sides of unit length are one and the square root of their sum is the square root of two which is 1.414.... See figure 10.

The two most famous irrational numbers are the square root of two and pi. It is very curious that both of these irrational numbers arise from geometrical ratios! The square root of two is a never ending decimal beginning with 1.414 and this is the length of the hypotenuse of a right triangle with sides of unit length. It is the ratio of the hypotenuse to a side. Pi arose from the discovery that

IRRATIONAL NUMBERS

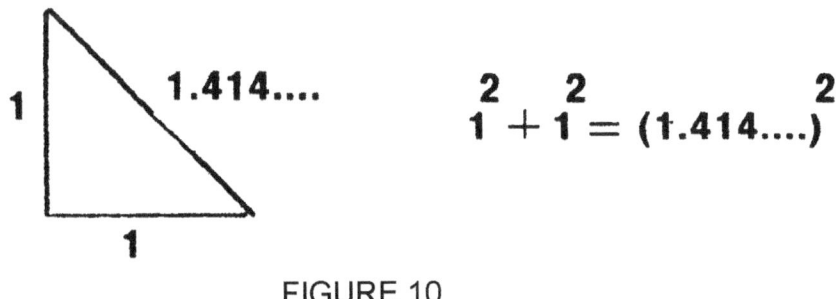

$$1^2 + 1^2 = (1.414....)^2$$

FIGURE 10

the ratio of the circumference of a circle to its diameter was not a rational number. Pi is a never-ending decimal beginning with 3.14159 and this is the length of the circumference of a circle with a diameter of unit length. See fig. 5.

Is it not curious that these two most fundamental geometric forms, these two geometrical ratios, should each lead to a consideration of irrational numbers? *Did pi have to be irrational?* Did that simplest of triangles *have to have an irrational number for a hypoteneuse?* Well, I guess it did!

Algebraic Equations

Algebraic equations are equations of the form $6x^2 + x-37 = 0$. x is an unknown quantity. In English the equation says, "To-37 add x and to that sum add six times x multiplied by x; then when the proper numerical value is substituted for x the total will be zero". In high school algebra we encountered "word problems" like: If John has twice as many apples as Jim and Jim has three times as many as Mary, and the total number of apples is ten, how many apples does Jim have? These kinds of problems lead to algebraic equations. (Poor Mary has only one apple).

Before we continue with our survey of numbers, and before we say goodbye to Pythagorus, we have to talk about the algebraic equations that represent an extension to the Pythagorean Theorem.

The Pythagorean theorem equation deals with a plane figure, a plane triangle, and we "square" each side, i.e. we multiply each side by itself, but suppose we want to deal with a three dimensional figure, that is to say with volumes instead of areas, then all the "squares" become "cubes". To find the volume of a geometrical cube of unit sides (i.e. each side = 1) we must multiply one by itself three times. This line of reasoning may very probably be the way in which "cubic equations" such as: $a^3=n$ arose. This particular equation is "of the third degree", in which a is the dimension of one side of a cube with volume equal to n (n cubic feet, n cubic yards, n cubic miles, n cubic amount of any dimension). When we deal only with numbers we need not identify any dimension). This simplest form of cubic equation appears in a Chinese book called The Nine Chapters in AD 263. Then, naturally, the study of equations of the third degree, cubic equations, led to study of equations of the fourth degree: (a)x(a)x(a)x(a)=n, which says 'a' multiplied by itself four times equals 'n'. This equation is written in mathematical notation as a^4=n; now the description of this as a fourth degree equation becomes clear. Cubic equations and equations of the fourth degree led to the study of equations of higher degree.

Algebraic equations are said to have "roots". Your calculator probably has a square root key, and if you paid enough to get more complex functionality it may help you to find cube roots and roots of higher degree. The equation (a)x(a)=1 (i.e. a^2 =1) asks the question "What number multiplied by itself equals one?". In mathematical jargon the same question asks, "What is the square root of 1?". The answer is that the square root of 1 is 1, but it is also-1; when each of these roots is "squared", i.e. multiplied by itself, the result is 1. Every positive number has two square roots, one plus, one minus, the square roots of four are 2 and-2, (2x2=4 and also (-2)x(-2)=4), the square roots of 100 are 10 and-10, and so on.

Algebraic equations have a number of roots and the number of these roots is equal to the degree of the equation; equations of degree two have two roots. As soon as the degree reaches three the roots will be threefold; there are four roots for equations of degree four, and so on. The degree of an algebraic equation is established by the number of times an unknown quantity is multiplied by itself: xx = x^2 is degree two; xxx = x^3 is degree three and so on. The equation x^4 = 256 is degree four and has four roots (x=4 is one root, 4x4x4x4=256; x =-4 is another, and there are two more!). Two of these roots will be "complex numbers" which involve the square root of-1. Be reminded; the square root of-1 is denoted by "i" and is called an **Imaginary Number**! Those ancestral mathematicians who first encountered this mathematical conundrum could not imagine a number which when multiplied by itself would equal-1. It was unbelievable! As a consequence the square roots of negative numbers were called "imaginary", an adjective which has, ever since, caused students of math who first encounter this adjective to go ballistic.

Remain seated. We shall soon deal with this mystery, and, although it will be a little painful, it is a truly fascinating subject without which our technological progress would have ceased long ago.

Negative numbers

After man had lost some of his early naivete, he *discovered* that extending the set of positive numbers with a set of negative numbers would simplify calculation. Negative numbers appear for the first time in China in the third century BC. Let's speculate on how this discovery might have happened.

Some ancient accountant was doing his sums when he asked himself, "What number would I have to add to 1 to make the 1 disappear?" We would say, "to make zero", but he almost certainly did not have a clear concept of zero. In algebraic terms he asked the question, "What value of x will satisfy the following equation: $1+x=0$". The answer, at that time, was by no means obvious because to assign a negative value to x requires two things: first the idea of "negativeness" and secondly an arithmetic indicator of its special nature. Our indicator today is the minus sign. The concept of adding a negative quantity is quite different from subtraction which is simply removing the 1. Whoever the Chinese gentleman may have been, he made a great discovery and must have been an extremely gifted mathematician.

Consequently we have the **Set of Negative Integers**. Add the set of positive integers and zero and we have **The Set of Positive and Negative Integers and Zero:**...-5,-4,-3,-2,-1,0,1,2,3,4,5...

Let's associate the positive and negative integers and zero with a straight line. See Figure11.

POSITIVE AND NEGATIVE INTEGERS, AND ZERO

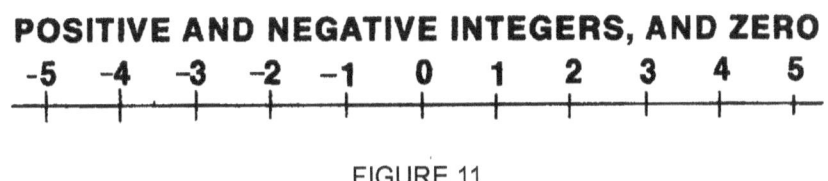

FIGURE 11

At the center of the line we will place zero, to the right of zero, at equal intervals, we will put the ascending positive integers and to the left of zero, at equal intervals, the descending negative integers. The numbers continue in both directions without end. This graphic way of representing all the integers will prove to be useful to us later. Let's pause for a moment and discuss the reasons, two in number, for all this emphasis on numbers. The first reason is that there are a lot of interesting, strange, "otherworldly" properties to the numbers we deal with so casually every day, as we have seen. These strange properties of items that are in themselves purely intellectual must intrigue and mystify us; why are these properties there? Is it just an accident or is it a key to some profound knowledge?

The second reason is that when mathematicians deal with the very most fundamental aspects of mathematics they must come back to the numbers. The numbers are the foundation, the "raison d'être" of all the rest of mathematics. If there is a mystery here to be solved it will be solved with the numbers. The most elegant, abstruse, arcane, and brain numbing aspects of math have to be justified by recourse to the numbers! **Any mathematical theorem has to work for all the numbers!** And there is an infinity of natural and rational numbers and there are more **Real Numbers** than there are natural and rational numbers.

What are the real numbers? (Most people think all numbers are real!) Well, there is a class of numbers that mathematicians have chosen to call "the real numbers" whether or not it makes sense. Get used to it, there is nothing you can do about it! The real numbers are all the numbers which can be expressed in a decimal expansion of infinite length. In any small interval, say between 1.000 and 1.001 there are an infinite number of real numbers, one of which is 1.0009999999999999999999...Consequently, between any two rational numbers, say 997/999 = 0.997997997...and 998/999 = 0.998998998...can be found an infinite number of real numbers; to quote Li'l Abner "as any fool can plainly see". If Li'l Abner's authority is insufficient be advised that a brilliant mathematician named Cantor proved that there are more real numbers than there are in the infinitely large set of rational numbers. *There are higher orders of infinity!* Now that is another *discovery* to add to our set of curiosities. And it is somewhat mind-boggling and really pretty doggoned curious! Think about it.

Well, if there are all these real numbers is there anything left? Yes, it is an unfortunate accident of history that this set of numbers has been given a name which has struck terror into the hearts of math students: **Complex Numbers**! They are our next mathematical subject, but to pave the way for these interesting fellows we first need to meet analytic geometry.

We are nearly at the end of our journey through number country; only complex numbers remain on our number agenda. What is the significance of what we have encountered in this journey? We have seen our ancestral Homo sapiens become conscious of oneness, twoness, threeness. He discovered tallying and then the sequence of numbers which he could associate with a row of articles, a row of beans. He learned that these numbers had very useful properties: addition, subtraction, multiplication and division. Then he learned that these bean identifiers had some unexpected and very strange properties: negative numbers and zero, prime numbers, Fibonocci's sequence and the Golden Ratio, irrational numbers, pi, imaginary numbers and many hidden surprises in perfect numbers, triangular numbers and many more. *Why does math go beyond simple arithmetic; at first glance what more would one expect from a row of beans; why is there such an exotic melange of properties associated with a numerical sequence?*

The mathematical toolbox is well supplied with basic tools. **Now we shall see how knowledge of the amazing properties of these numbers,**

knowledge acquired with such great difficulty and over an enormous time span, opens the gates to an understanding of nature.

While the Europeans were making dramatic progress in mathematics and the natural sciences, what was happening across the Atlantic? Let's pause for a moment to see what has happened in the New World. Perhaps we shall discover that the inhabitants of the two American continents have outdistanced their Old World fellows in math and science. What role have they been destined to play in the evolution of Homo sapiens?

Then we shall return to the Old World as Descartes discovers analytic geometry.

Chapter Six

The New World

While Europe, Asia Minor, and Asia were progressing with science and mathematics, what was happening in the vast reaches of North and South America? Genus Homo sapiens had found his way to these continents; there is no reason to believe that parallel discoveries in math and science would escape the large brains of these cousins of the Europeans. Surely nature had endowed all equally with intelligence. Perhaps these isolated societies would progress in mathematics and the sciences well beyond those of the Old World.

But the New World was barren of all but the most elementary math and science. Was the Creator responsible for this dichotomy? Did he have a reason for disclosing math and science to one set of Homo sapiens while denying them to another? Is it just an accident that, over a time span of centuries, one set of people should discover these keys to the natural world while an equivalent set did not? *This is an extremely curious, puzzling and unexpected historical fact.* Is it possible that the two isolated societies were predestined to play different roles in Homo sapiens' development?

Perhaps the fifteenth century occupants of the New World were to play the role of custodians; to establish a set of conditions on the two continents that would prepare the way for those who would bring to America a unique set of political and governmental concepts, the keys to a free society? A free society which could exploit the mathematical and scientific discoveries of the Old World for the benefit of all. Should we be searching for a pattern of celestial intervention in the sequence of events which occurred? What does the history of the New World tell us that might illuminate this question?

The Mal'ta

The first visitors to the New World came from Asia. There is evidence now that at least some of these migrants came across the Bering Strait from two regions in Siberia, but they are believed to have migrated to those two Siberian regions from the general area of Lake Baikal. During the Ice Age much of the global water in the oceans had been frozen and the water level was as much as 400 feet lower than it is today. Consequently the Bering Strait was transformed into open tundra several hundred miles wide and it undoubtedly supported abundant game. As growing human populations in Asia were accompanied by reductions in the population of local game, hungry people were pushed eastward along the wide Strait into Alaska. From Alaska they roamed into the rest of North America. Anthropologists believe these migrants came to the New World as much as 20,000-25,000 years ago and that they continued their migration south until, about ten thousand years ago, they reached the southern tip of South America. The migrants were probably members of a peripatetic group of Asians known as the Mal'ta. The Mal'ta were mammoth hunters who are known to have occupied the Lake Baikal area about 20,000 years ago. There appear to be similarities among the weapons and tools of the Mal'ta and those of Native Americans. The Asian immigrants spread eastward as well as southward; some of them reached Pennsylvania more than 16,000 years ago. At Meadowcroft, not far from Pittsburgh, there is evidence of a settlement that dates to that time.

How can anthropologists trace to an Asian origin the ancestry of natives of North and South America? They study DNA mutations as a clue to population migrations; they are a new breed known as "molecular anthropologists". Unlike the story of Eve, this is a story of Adams. There are certain markers on the Y chromosomes of a large percentage of a large sample of Native American men; these markers are common to the markers of Asian men from the two Siberian regions. These markers unmistakably give these two population groups a common ancestry! Some anthropologists believe that there were also Polynesian and perhaps Japanese migrants to the New World who came by sea; it remains for the molecular anthropologist to confirm or refute this speculation.

In some parts of the two New World continents the pattern of transformation from hunter-gatherer bands to an agricultural based society followed the European pattern. Large societies and sophisticated cultures developed in Mexico, Central America and northern South America. As in Europe and Asia there were large and fertile areas surrounding the large rivers. The Nile, Euphrates, Ganges and Yellow rivers had their parallels in the Mississippi, the Missouri, the Colorado, the Parana, the Amazon and the other great rivers of the two continents. But Homo sapiens' development of an understanding of nature seems to have stopped at the continental limits. There is little evidence that more than a primitive mathematics and writing appeared anywhere on the two continents! A settlement known as Cahokia near the confluence of the Mississippi, Missouri and Illinois rivers flourished in an area called the American Bottoms. It reached a population peak estimated at 38,000, but apart from some circles of wooden post-holes suggesting observations of the solstices and equinox there is no evidence of anything like a primitive science. Cahokia was abandoned and had disappeared by the end of the 14th century.

Why was the development of math and science progressing in Egypt, Mesopotamia, India, Greece and China, but not among the inhabitants of the New World? Surely there was no great difference in the mental abilities of the people in the Americas. Why was math discovered only in the Old World, and why did it flourish later, during the 17th, 18th, and 19th centuries, only in Western Europe? Why did the Western Europeans dominate the immigration to America? Was it on reserve for them? And to what end?

The Vikings

Following the Asian migrants the next group of visitors to the New World, or temporary migrants, were the Scandinavian Vikings. They were explorers of the first rank; their discoveries progressed from the Faeroes to Iceland to Greenland and ultimately to North America.

Eric the Red was the Norwegian son of a Viking named Thorvald. Thorvald had killed a man in a brawl and had been convicted of manslaughter; he was exiled from Norway and sailed for Iceland with young Eric. When Eric reached manhood he married Thjodhild who bore him three sons. He also sired a daughter who was born on the wrong side of the blanket. A true son of his father, Eric dispatched two men to Valhalla in an Icelandic dustup and was banished from the island. After his exile from Iceland on charges of manslaughter, Eric the Red led a group of adventurers west in 982 AD and discovered a land which he named Greenland. His choice of this misnomer for a frigid ice-capped island was a successful effort to deceive and persuade Icelandic adventurers to settle this new land. In 985 nearly 1000 people, together with their domestic animals (which were about half the size of the domestic animals we raise today) set sail in a couple of dozen small boats for Greenland. About half of their number were lost at sea or turned back, the other half arrived safely and established a settlement.

Eric's second son, Leif Ericsson, discovered Newfoundland, which he called Vinland. He established a settlement there, of that history is sure. (Curious artifacts which might be of Viking origin have been discovered as far afield as New England, Minnesota, Tennessee, and Oklahoma. Some scholars believe that the Vikings found their way to these distant areas. Of this history is not sure). Under Leif's leadership Newfoundland was settled by a band of these Norsemen who began trading with Greenland and also with the Skraelings (natives).

For a time things progressed tranquilly at Vinland. Then Leif's sister, Freydis, who was as big and strong as a man, added to Vinland's colorful history. Freydis had made an agreement with two Viking brothers to load her ship and theirs with trade goods, timber and furs, at Vinland, then, for the sake of safety, sail together to Greenland. These goods, especially the timber, would be extremely valuable in Greenland for there was no timber there. The brothers' ship was larger than Freydis' and she wanted it very badly, so she decided to offer to buy it. One dewy night she came to one of the brothers with an offer that included more than money. Caught by her husband with wet clothing which aroused his suspicions, she persuaded husband Thorvard to gather his cohorts and kill the brothers and all their men whom she falsely accused of using her badly. The men were killed, but there remained five wives who were witnesses to the mayhem. Thorvard and his men were unwilling to kill the women. Then, to seal their lips, Freydis dispatched the five wives to Valhalla with an axe! Now she had the brothers' ship at no charge!

In addition to being a rough, rugged and bloodthirsty lot the Norsemen were very competent sailors; they employed "latitude sailing" together with their knowledge of the ocean environment. Birds, marine life, ocean currents, prevailing winds were all navigational clues which supported their use of the stars to tell them how far north they were, i.e. at what latitude. The angle subtended by the North Star above the horizon was a measure of their latitude, so was the elevation of the sun at midday, adjusted for the season. They would sail a course west, keeping the elevation of the North Star and the midday sun constant as they went, and then, as they returned east, these stellar friends brought them home to Norway.

By 1020 the Vikings abandoned Newfoundland as a consequence of hostility on the part of the Skraelings (they killed Leif's brother). By the end of the 14th century the Norsemen had also abandoned Greenland.

In the period following the Viking abandonment of Newfoundland and Greenland, knowledge of a land to the southwest of Greenland was lost. However, there is a story that a young Italian sailor visited Iceland about 1477 and heard from Icelandic sailors rumors of a mysterious land to the west. His name was Cristoforo Columbo.

The history of the New World would be very different had the Vikings stayed the course, developed their foothold in Newfoundland and expanded to the balance of the North American continent. Sailors and adventurers that they were, it seems very curious that they did not sail south and explore the eastern shore of the continent. Why were they intimidated by the Indians; they had encountered much more sophisticated adversaries in their European wars and conquests? One might ask if they were a glitch in some grander plan for the New World. As we shall see, we shall be motivated to ask again and again why the history of the United States evolved as it did. Why?

The Spaniards

Cristopher Columbus writes the next chapter in the discovery of the New World. As we all know, his discovery was an accident, since he expected to find a trade route to India (and caused Native Americans to be mis-labeled as a result). Why in heaven's name did Columbus believe India and the Orient lay across the Atlantic? Because he was misled by Ptolemy! Ptolemy (121-157 AD) was a geographer as well as an astronomer; as an astronomer he made an enormous astronomical error when he pronounced that the earth was the center of the universe. As a geographer he made a similar mistake in pronouncing that the circumference of the earth was 18,000 miles, about 7,000 miles short of the correct value. Ptolemy's pronouncements were the voice of authority more than a millenium after he made them! Columbus studied the ancient maps and made a very rational surmise that by sailing a reasonable distance to the west he would encounter India. Is this not strange? We know that Eratosthenes had made a very accurate estimate of the earth's circumference, in a very understandable way, long before Ptolemy walked the earth.

If Eratosthenes' number had prevailed Columbus might very probably have been discouraged in his adventure by the enormous distance across the ocean to India. Very strange! Just a typical human foible of listening to the wrong authority? Or was it necessary for Columbus to do what he did as the first step in a mission for the New World? Did someone cook the historical books?

Shortly after Columbus' famous voyage in 1492 his fellow Spaniards were plundering Mexico, Central America and Peru. Balboa discovered the Pacific Ocean in 1513. Thirty years later the Spanish mariners had sailed the West Coast from Panama to Oregon and south to the northern part of South America.

Hernando Cortez' (1485-1547) first adventure in the New World was to participate, under the direction of Diego Velasquez, in the conquest of Cuba. Velasquez subsequently became governor of Cuba. When Mexico was discovered in 1517 Velasquez authorized an expedition of Mexican exploration under the leadership of Cortez. Landing on Mexican soil in March of 1519, Cortez took numerous captives; one of whom became his mistress, interpreter and advisor. From the captives he learned of the Aztec empire and king Montezuma. Allied with native enemies of Montezuma, Cortez entered the Aztec capital as a god; his white skin and black beard resonated with an ancient prediction of such a god. He was unopposed. To secure his situation, Cortez took Montezuma captive and he became Cortez' puppet. The Spaniards mistreated the natives, and not long after Cortez' arrival the Aztecs revolted against Montezuma and the cruel Spaniards. During the revolt Montezuma was killed by his subjects and Cortez was ejected from the capital city. A little later still, Cortez returned, retook the capital, razed it and it became Mexico City, the principal European city in North America at that time.

Voyages under the direction of Cortez and Antonio de Mendoza, the first colonial viceroy in Mexico, explored the Pacific coast seeking treasure. Motivated by rumors of riches to be found at The Seven Cities and The Amazon Island, these two established bases at Zacatula and Navidad to support maritime exploration and exploitation of Mexico and the region to the north. (The Amazon Island was reported to be inhabited solely by women who reproduced "in the way which the ancient histories ascribe to the amazons").

In 1540 Mendoza established the Coronado expedition which explored the lower Colorado river country, discovered the Grand Canyon and probed as far eastward as central Kansas. Mendoza sent another expedition north by sea under the command of Juan Rodriguez Cabrillo. Cabrillo ranged north up the California coast; he discovered San Diego Bay, but missed Monterey Bay and the Golden Gate.

The exploration of the southwestern part of what is now the United States was well under way. The exploration of the northwestern part waited nearly three centuries for Lewis and Clark.

The Spanish focused their efforts on the search for gold and other treasure. They decimated the indigent population. They failed as a colonizing power. Why did they fail? Were they destined to fail so that the English could succeed?

The English

Shortly after Columbus' successful voyage of discovery there were follow-up voyages of discovery mounted by Spain, Portugal, and France. All of these explorations were aimed at plundering the riches of the New World, and all of the New World was "up for grabs". The Spanish focused their attention on Mexico and the riches of the Aztecs; the Portugese focused on Peru and the riches of the Incas, and the French focused on the marine riches of the Grand Banks and subsequently on Canada. The natives of what is now the United States were still hunter-gatherers; they had no riches and once this was ascertained this area was largely ignored.

Sugar and silver were the first New World treasures to be exploited. The exploitation called for mines and sugar plantations, and the mines and plantations needed labor. In the absence of an abundant and cooperative indigenous population, slaves were needed to provide the labor. In the mid-fifteenth century the Portugese had discovered the riches to be found in supplying slave labor to plantations in the islands offshore of southern Europe and Africa; so they began a large scale exploitation of the human resources of black Africa. The Portugese slave trade grew; it supplied slaves to much of Europe and to all of the plantations of the New World. Slavery was an ancient practice in Africa as captives taken in tribal wars were enslaved by local chieftains, but the Portugese added their own touch of savagery and inhumanity to slavery. Their colony in Brazil became the center of an infamous, large and cruel slave trade.

In the midst of the competition for the richest areas of the New World the real treasure house was unrecognized. It consisted of the rich and fertile soil, the abundant water, the natural mineral resources and the moderate temperature of the area north of the Caribbean and south of Canada. Almost no one was interested until the English came. There were abortive initial attempts by the English and others to create settlements along the East coast. The lost settlement of Roanoke is the best-known example. The first settlement to take hold was Jamestown.

In 1607 the Jamestown colony was established; it would turn out to be the first viable English settlement in America. One of the settlers, John Rolfe, is notable for three reasons: he married an Indian princess, Pocahontas, he developed the first exportable tobacco and he noted in his diary the importation of the first group of 20 black laborers, slaves in all but name. The year was 1619; the next year the Mayflower landed at Plymouth.

The settlers that landed from the Mayflower sought relief from coercion in their religious beliefs; in the new land they would be able to believe whatever they chose to believe without pressure from the English Church or the English government. They were self-righteous, ultra-conservative idealists who would brook no nonsense, but they were also industrious and energetic people. The settlers at Jamestown, on the other hand, were of more of a liberal cut; fair-minded, reasonable Englishmen who believed that the law should apply equally to all. Both of these colonies were far from the English throne and were faced with the problem of self-government in a form that served the common interest. In a sense, all were in the same boat, and that boat was of necessity a democratic one. They solved their governmental problem with laws and authority which derived from the consent of the governed. Liberty was the watchword, individual liberty. To the Puritans, Liberty and God were inseparable. Our coins say even today "in God we trust" in one area of the primary face and "Liberty" across the top. The Virginians were Good Christians of the kind who could countenance a sometimes brutal slavery in support of the riches that tobacco brought to them. Diverging roads were established by these two settlements: one accepted the practice of slavery; the other did not. This ethical difference would eventually threaten the new republic.

Is it not strange that the roots of the United States were established by groups of English settlers whose tenets were Liberty, Equality under the Law, Morality as embodied in the Christian religion, and Economic Opportunity for all? And that these ideas would be supported by a huge, rich and abundant land that could permit a great republic to grow from those roots? These settlers came to build a better life, not to plunder or enslave the indigents. Would the Spaniards or French have founded the same kind of society; or would the country now resemble Mexico or Quebec? Why were those members of the English who believed so whole-heartedly in liberty, religious freedom and the rule of law the ones to set the future course of the United States? The world of today would be a very different place had this bit of history been different. *Did some cosmic hand want it to be the way it is?*

Throughout all of the colonies building that better life involved an aggressive pursuit of the abundant cheap land which was the wealth of the new economy. In the South the aggressive pursuit of cheap labor to work the enormously profitable tobacco plantations called for the importation of African slaves. The newcomers to America did not plunder the treasure of the indigents (who had none to plunder) nor did they enslave them, but they did eject them from their lands. Assisting the immigrants in their efforts to dispossess the Indians was the scourge of smallpox which decimated many tribal populations. Syphilis and other venereal diseases imported from Europe did their bit to disable the natives too. On the positive side of the ledger, the immigrants discarded the centuries-long traditions of European nobles, privileged classes and serfs and erected a system of social and governmental equality. This system was based on individual liberty and on common law that applied equally to all. The law was established by the consent of those to whom it applied. The administration of government was the responsibility of elected officials in America in dramatic contrast to the appointed officials in England.

In Virginia and the South the plantations gave rise to a leisure class of landed gentry; in Massachusetts and New England, where there were no plantations, there arose a hard-working class of Yankees. Different as they were, these two groups shared the same standards of liberty under the law. By the mid-1700's the shared values of the colonies became much more important than the competitive and ethical differences which separated them. The colonial citizens now thought of themselves as Americans. They were Americans who readily acknowledged that they were subject to British authority, but more and more they saw America and Britain as equals. The British, on the other hand, saw America as inferior, as a weak, divided and often unruly colonial possession; they did not hesitate to levy unfair taxes and other burdens. In 1763 a Royal Proclamation reserved the land beyond the existing frontier to the Indians! This would have terminated American growth! The Proclamation was ignored by the colonists. More and more, the Americans, who were treated like second-class citizens, chafed under the ill-advised laws imposed on them from abroad and were irritated with their masters across the Atlantic. The Boston Teaparty was an act of rebellion against unreasonable taxation. Next, the British forcibly quartered some of their troops with families in Boston. Then the Boston port was closed to all marine operations. Americans believed they were facing the loss of their liberty and the rule of law. The stage was set for rebellion and war. The first shots were fired on April 19th near Lexington and Concord after the famous midnight ride of Paul Revere. The Revolutionary War had begun.

At this time a remarkable group of men emerged from the various colonies: Washington from Virginia, Franklin from Pennsylvania, Adams from Massachusetts, Jefferson, Hamilton, Madison and many more of great talent and dedication to the new country. They were full of energy and courage. They were loyal to each other and ready to pledge to the new nation and to each other: "Our Lives, our Fortunes and our sacred Honor".

George Washington was elected Commander in Chief of the infant American Continental Army. For more than a year, hoping to reconcile their differences with the mother-country, the leaders of the American colonies avoided a split with Britain. Then, on June 11, 1776, their patience exhausted, the members of the Continental Congress appointed Franklin, Adams, Jefferson, Roger Sherman and Robert Livingston to a committee charged with developing a Declaration of Independence. Jefferson did the heavy lifting. His "life, liberty and the pursuit of happiness" will echo through the corridors of time forever. On July 4,1776 the Declaration of Independence was adopted by all thirteen colonies. On July 8th it was read publicly in the State House Yard in Philadelphia, and the pealing of the Liberty Bell announced to the world the birth of a new nation.

The new American nation was a loose federation of thirteen colonies: Massachusetts, New Hampshire, Rhode Island, Connecticut, New York, Pennsylvania, New Jersey, Maryland, Delaware, Virginia, North Carolina, South Carolina and Georgia. They all recognized the need for a common set of governmental rules; how was America to be governed as an entity? Delegates from all thirteen states (former colonies) met in Convention in 1787 to address this problem. On September 17, 1787 they had composed a set of rules that reflected the experiences of each colony with individual liberty, equality, and common law. They had settled their disagreements by compromise. Their labors brought forth The United

States Constitution! Madison was the principal architect with a strong assist from Hamilton but with participation by all the delegates to the Convention. It was a remarkable achievement and a testimony to the intelligence and fair-mindedness of all the delegates. There was a last minute hitch, the founding fathers had a great fear of Big Government, and insisted that, after ratification by the states, the first order of business would be to amend the Constitution with a Bill of Rights which would protect individual liberties. By May of 1790 all thirteen states had ratified and the Constitution was law. In December of 1791 the Bill of Rights was ratified and joined the Constitution. A miraculous system of self-government established the new Republic on a fast-track toward the future!

How did this wonderful opportunity to build a democratic society, blind to ethnic and racial differences with liberty and equality for all, happen? The building may be incomplete 200 years later, but the opportunity is still there and the structure is being erected, more slowly than we might wish, but steadily, none-the-less. Was this remarkable beginning just an accident? Why does it seem that the North American continent had been reserved for this new nation? Why was the new nation a beacon for the oppressed; why did it hold out its arms, a refuge for the hopeless, downtrodden hordes of Europe: "Give me your tired, your poor, your huddled masses yearning to breathe free"? Why did it rescue Europe on three occasions without any reward? What do you think?

There is more. Jefferson and Adams, the co-writers of the Declaration of Independence, were first comrades, then enemies, and then, in their old age, friends again. John Adams was eight years senior to Jefferson and appears to have been jealous of young Jefferson's notoriety as sole author of the Declaration when both had contributed to its creation. This began a split which grew as Jefferson, who was Adams' Vice President, differed with Adams on political issues. Then, after Jefferson retired in 1809, the two men carried on a lengthy and friendly correspondence in their old age. John Adams died on July 4, 1826, exactly fifty years after the adoption of the Declaration of Independence! Thomas Jefferson died July 4,

1826, **the same day as John Adams**! Ask a mathematician for the probability that this can be a chance occurrence: that two old patriots (key founders of the Republic), the second and third Presidents of the United States, co-framers of the Declaration of Independence, should *both* die on the fiftieth anniversary of the day their Declaration was adopted! Can this be only a coincidence? Or might we hope that some celestial power arranged for them to march through the Pearly Gates together? It boggles the mind!

The fledgling republic encountered many hurdles as it ran toward its destiny: Slavery, Civil War, the acquisition of Florida, the territory that separated it from the Pacific Ocean, the transformation from an agricultural to an industrial economy, the Melting Pot society which absorbed all racial and ethnic groups, various experiments with Social Engineering, World War One, World War Two and the Cold War. In all three of these wars America was the deciding factor, it contributed the blood of its young men and the treasure of the country to put down despotic forces from across the oceans. With the Marshall Plan it restored its vanquished enemies to prosperity. Never before had the Victor spurned the spoils of war.

Many problems remain in the American society. These challenges are being surmounted slowly but surely, one by one, in the tradition set by the founding fathers: Liberty, Equality under the Common Law, Opportunity for those who will seize it, and a basic fair-mindedness and good will toward all men. Is there any similar society on the planet or in history? *Is this American experience just an accident, or will America lead Homo sapiens toward an unknown destiny?*

While the explosion of the population of the United States was under way west of the Atlantic, the mathematical explosion in 17th century Europe continued unabated. We return to the European revelations in math and science with a look at Analytic Geometry.

Chapter Seven

Analytic Geometry

Analytic Geometry and its partner, complex numbers, are the foundation on which the calculus is built, and it is the calculus that provides the marvelous tools which enable us to understand the physics of nature. We shall learn a little about the fundamentals of the calculus in Chapter Eight; then we shall see a few of its applications reveal to us some of the astounding ways in which nature behaves. In this chapter we shall build the foundation,

Analytic geometry is the application of algebra to the mathematics of geometry. Analytic geometry enables mathematicians to express geometrical figures in algebraic terms (equations) and to express algebraic equations in geometrical terms (figures). The invention (*discovery*) of analytic geometry on November 10, 1619 is attributed to a Frenchman named Rene Descartes. Descartes reported that analytic geometry was revealed to him in the second of three mystical dreams that occurred on Saint Martin's Eve after an evening of feasting and drinking. (Descartes professes that for him it was an evening of sobriety!). Whether the dream was indeed a revelation from some cosmic source or, instead, an overtaxed liver, the consequences to the human race were huge.

Descartes was a curious mix of scientist, philosopher, mathematician and theologian. He lived at the time of the Inquisition and was devastated at the fate of Galileo, a contemporary, who was forced on his knees to renounce the Copernican theory that the earth revolves around the sun. Descartes was a devout Catholic and believed in both the infallibility of the Pope and the theory of Copernicus. Caught in this contradiction he delayed publishing his findings until June 8, 1637 when analytic geometry was revealed. In 1664 the Catholic Church placed Descartes on the Index (a list of forbidden books created by the Roman Catholic Church), but by the turn of the century interest in his work was widespread.

Analytic geometry is the rootstock of the calculus, for it provides a solution to the problem of finding the tangent at any point of a curved, continuous line lying completely in a plane. Finding the tangent to a curve is the way in which mathematicians determine rates of change of one quantity with respect to another quantity.

For example, if we record the temperature of a room at every minute of the day; we can use analytic geometry to determine the number of degrees per minute that the temperature is changing at any particular time (i.e. the rate of change of the room temperature with respect to time). To do this we make a graph of Room Temperature vs Time (Figure 12). To mathematicians the graph is known as a "curve", even if it is a straight line! The tangent to any point on that curve will tell us the rate at which the room temperature is changing with respect to time at the time represented by the point on the curve. Velocity is the rate of change of distance with time; your bank account increases at a rate which depends on the interest rate and the time, and so on.

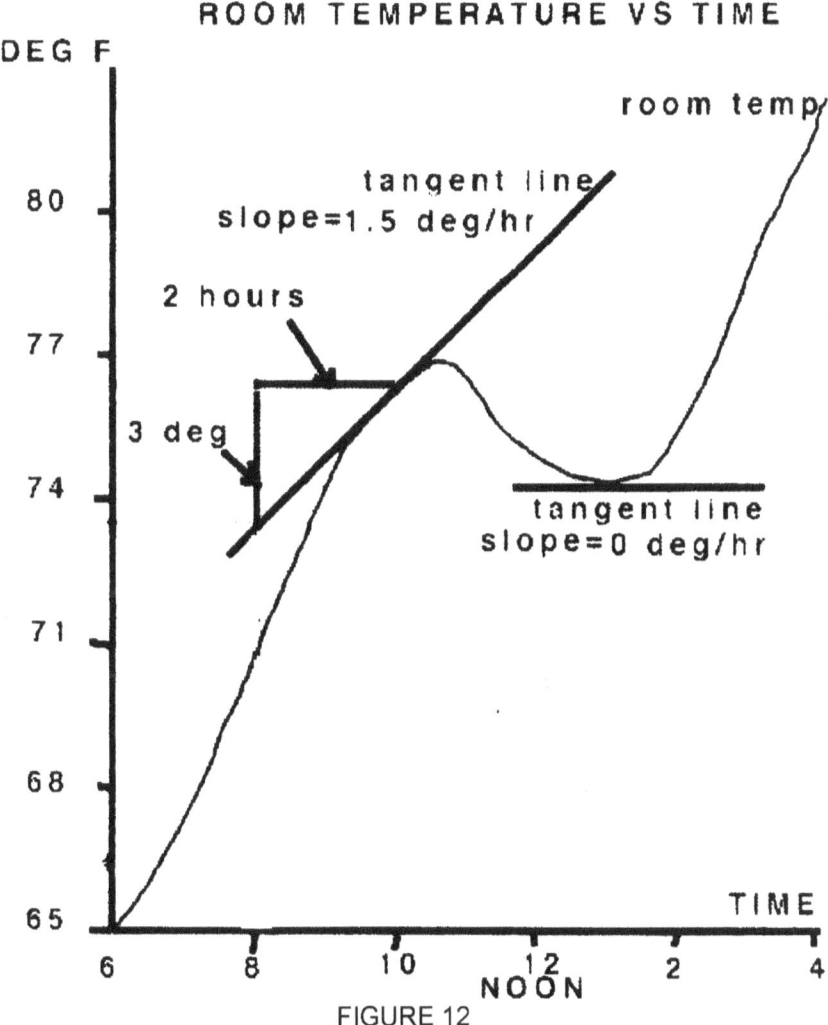

ROOM TEMPERATURE VS TIME

FIGURE 12

The differential calculus solves the problem of finding rates of change; the integral calculus solves the problem of finding the area of any plane geometric figure. These two fundamental problems are solved with the aid of analytic geometry.

Until the discovery of analytic geometry mathematics was a math of the "discrete" as distinct from the "continuous", and this placed a severe limitation on analysis. The "discreteness" arises from the inability to find a limit to the process of dividing a line into smaller and smaller pieces. Mathematically, one can take a line of finite length and assign a natural number to each millimeter of its length; then, one may divide each millimeter length into ten parts increasing the number of natural numbers assigned to the line by ten. This process can be repeated as often as we choose and there will still be a finite, though tiny, dimension to each segment of the line. In this mathematical sense the line is made up of discrete parts, it is not "continuous". Eudoxus, in the fourth century BC, conceived of making the residual segment "as small as we please", but it remained for Fermat, Newton and Leibniz to proceed to the limit of an infinite number of segments of zero length and thereupon discover the concept of the continuous.

Newton and Leibniz are responsible for the concept of the product of two quantities one of which increases toward infinity and the other of which decreases toward zero while the product remains unchanged. (Mathematically a product is the result of multiplying two numbers together: 2x3=6; 6 is the product. Let the first number, 2, be the increasing number and the second, 3, be the decreasing number. Then 20x0.3 = 6; 200x0.03 = 6, 2000x 0.003 = 6 and so on.). See Fig. 13.

DELTA FUNCTION

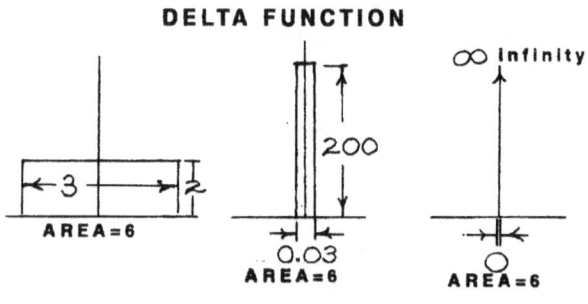

Figure 13

This concept has proved to be an invaluable tool to mathematical physicists, one of whom (an Englishman named P.A.M. Dirac, of whom more later) called a similar quantity a "delta function" early in the twentieth century. The delta function has played a prominent role in modern quantum physics, in quantum electrodynamics.

Analytic Geometry has the beauty of great simplicity, never-the-less, it is the framework within which many very sophisticated and complex problems can be solved because it relates algebraic equations and curved lines lying in a plane! Prior to Analytic Geometry mathematicians concentrated most of their attention on lines and the division of lines into tiny segments; now they are dealing with a plane and its division into tiny areas. The next step is three dimensional with a volume divided into tiny cubes, and so on to four or more dimensions.[*] Analytic Geometry permits the mathematician to visualize concepts by providing a picture in two dimensions that illustrates his problem when it is expressed in an algebraic equation involving the relationship between two changing quantities (variables to the mathematician). For example, the flight of an airplane moving at constant speed covers a changing distance (the first variable) given by the product of the constant speed and the increasing time (the second variable). The algebraic equation relating these two quantities is:

$y = s\,t$ where y = distance; s = constant speed and t = time.

A straightforward extension to three (and even more) dimensions permits mental visualization of problems involving three or more variables.

---

[*]As an example of many variables consider the temperature, pressure, and humidity at any point in a room of three dimensions: six variables.

Modern computers use the concepts of analytic geometry to show "3 D" images of buildings and other solid objects on the computer screen by mapping any view of the three dimensional object, i.e. the view of an observer at any location relative to the object, onto a two dimensional plane. Contour lines or highlights enhance the effect.

Analytic Geometry permits the geometer to analyze any geometric figure in algebraic/numerical terms as distinct from attempting an analysis, as the Greeks did, with compass and ruler. (The Greek ruler had no markings; it was simply a straightedge). Therefore the analytic geometer requires an algebraic description of a plane geometric figure. The figure may be a circle, a straight line or any curve drawn in the plane. How does the mathematician accomplish this? First he constructs a grid on which to draw his figure. Refer to Fig. 14.

ANALYTIC GEOMETRY GRID

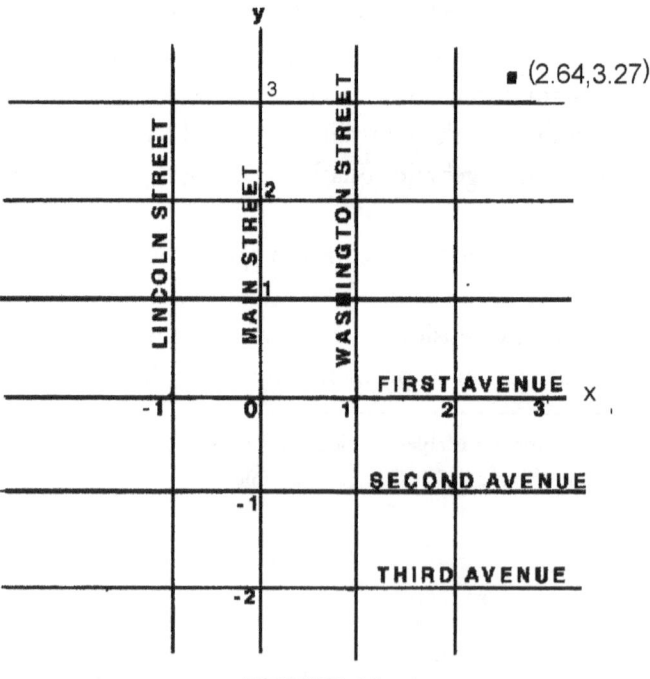

FIGURE 14

Take two straight lines lying in a plane on a piece of paper that intersect at a right angle. (Imagine Main Street and First Avenue intersecting at right angles as they do in most American Cities, and imagine furthermore that Main Street runs north and south and First Avenue east and west). Mark each line on the piece of paper at intervals (say, one inch apart), and assign a progression of positive integers (1,2,3,...) to the interval marks going north along the Main Street line, which we shall call the positive Y axis, and a progression of positive integers (1,2,3,...) to the interval marks going east along the First Avenue line, which we shall call the positive X axis, and a progression of negative integers (-1,-2,-3...) to the interval marks going south, the negative Y axis, and also to those going west, the negative X axis. Associate the number zero (0) with the intersection of the two lines (the corner of Main and First).

The two intersecting lines together with the numbers marking intervals on them is called a Cartesian Coordinate System. See Figure 14.

Imagine grid lines at each interval mark (Second Ave., Third Ave.,...and Washington Street, Lincoln Street,...) which are parallel to the respective X and Y axes (First Ave. and Main Street). These grid lines divide the plane up into a number of small squares (city blocks in our analogy). Any point in the plane can be identified by two decimal numbers: **The Address** of the point; one the shortest distance from the Y axis (i.e. the x distance) and the other the shortest distance from the X axis (i.e. y). These two numbers are called the coordinates (i.e. the address) of the point and are typically given x first and then, separated by a comma, y; for example if x=2.64 and y=3.27, (x,y) would be (2.64,3.27). Often letters will be used instead of numbers in examples: (a,b) etc. where the two letters a,b can take on different number values. (We are reminded of the grid lines on the surface of the earthly sphere which mark longitude and latitude, see Figure 4).

The "Cartesian" coordinate system we have just described is the basic tool of Analytic Geometry; it permits any algebraic equation relating x and y to be drawn as a curve on a piece of paper. The other side of that coin is that any curve drawn on a piece of paper can be defined by an algebraic equation. x is usually taken as the "independent variable", in other words the value of x is used to determine the value of y rather than vice-versa. If the equation were y=6x and we choose x = 2 then y = 12 and so on.

Let's consider a simple application of analytic geometry. Imagine the flight of a bee over a large plane piece of paper. See Figure 15.

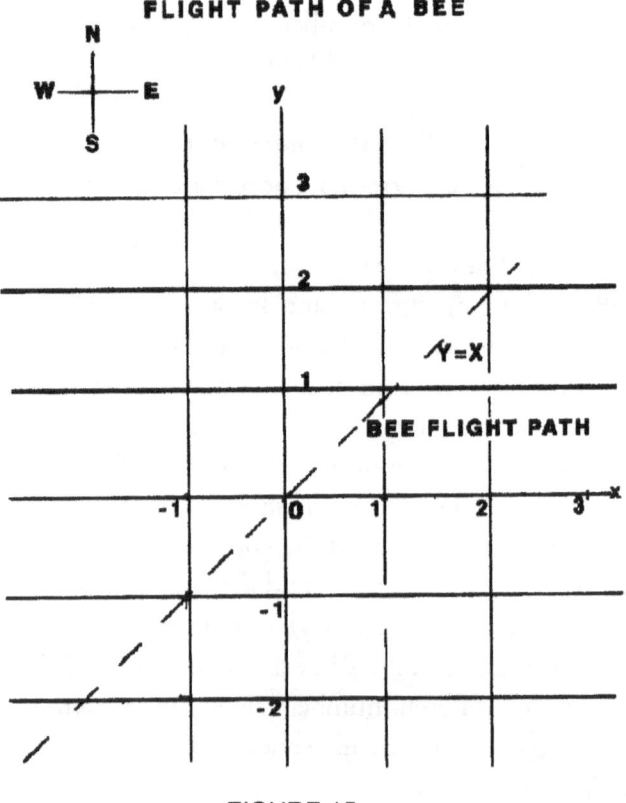

FIGURE 15

There is a Cartesian coordinate system drawn on the piece of paper. The time is noon sharp. The sun is directly overhead. The bee's shadow will trace out a curved irregular line on the piece of paper and to every point (x,y) of the curve a pair of numbers, an address, (a,b) can be assigned. Now, an algebraic equation can be written for any curve that has been traced out by the bee's flight. For simplicity's sake let's take a bee who is homing to the hive in a very straight line. The bee is flying northeast; his flight path is equidistant from the x axis and the y axis (from Main Street and from First Avenue) a flight path for which y=x. The bee is flying diagonally across the grid squares (city blocks). When y=2, x=2; when y=5, x=5. The "curve" representing the bee's flight is a straight line equidistant from the X and Y axes. But *any* flight path of the bee and any algebraic equation relating x and y, will trace out a curve in the plane; whatever the value of x there will be a corresponding value of y. The equation for this bee's flight is y=x.

Let's see what curves a few algebraic expressions trace out in the plane. See Fig. 16.

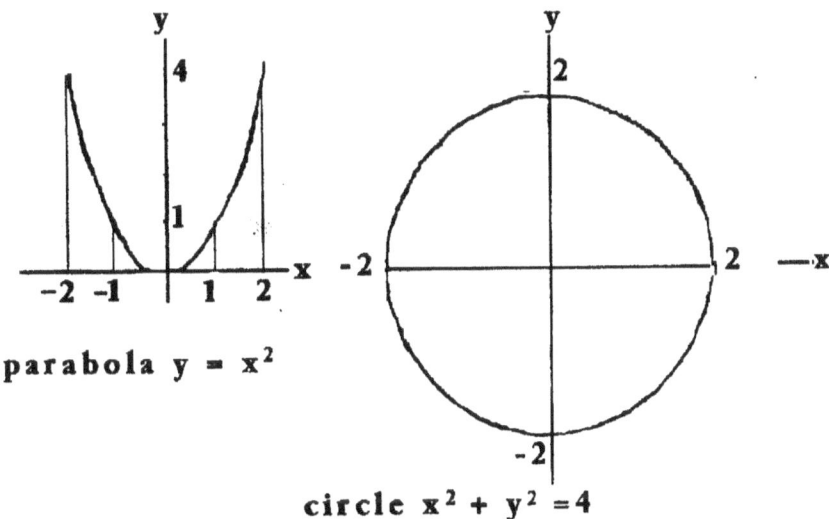

parabola y = x²

circle x² + y² = 4

Figure 16

Complex Numbers

There is a simple extension to what we have encountered thus far, but the extension has a somewhat sobering name: **Complex Numbers**! The term may be intimidating, but the mathematical utility of complex numbers is awesome.

Why are complex numbers important? Complex numbers enable the analysis of many physical problems which would be immune to other branches of mathematics. Complex numbers are essential to the analysis of electrical circuits and the design of electrical machines; work performed by electrical engineers. They are fundamental to the analysis of fluid flow in a plane; for example, in determining the non-turbulent flow-pattern of water flowing past an obstruction. Complex quantities are fundamental to the quantum mechanics of physics. It is quantum mechanics which enables us to understand the tiny world of the atom and its nucleus. The very well-spring of modern quantum mechanics, which is called the Schroedinger equation, involves complex variables and complex number concepts.

Complex numbers have two parts, one of the parts is a "real" number, the second is an "imaginary" number. We encountered imaginary numbers in Chapter Five; they involve the square root of a (-1) in combination with a real number. For example "ib" where "i" is the square root of-1 and "b" is any real number.

A complex number has the form: a+ib. "a" designates a real number and "ib" designates an imaginary number. When a and b take on different values the complex number is called a "complex variable". The use of complex variables is essential to the solution of many important mathematical problems. A complex variable is usually designated by z=x+iy where x and y can take on variable values. Complex numbers are of great importance in mathematics because they open the door to the analysis of some very practical but sophisticated problems (for example, the flow of air over the airfoil form of an airplane wing). They also open up a whole new domain of mathematics.

However, this new form of number has one great drawback! Now we have lost the ability to establish a one-to-one correspondence with that helpful one-dimensional row of beans; instead, we establish a correspondence with a two-dimensional position in a plane using analytic geometry. But, hold on a moment; perhaps if we lay our beans out in the form of a cross with real beans laid along the x axis and imaginary beans laid along the y axis of our Cartesian Grid we can rescue the concept! Then a point a+ib in the plane will be found opposite the "a" bean on the x axis and the "ib" bean on the y axis.

Where did these esoteric complex fellows come from and who developed the mathematics they make possible? Sixteenth century mathematicians encountered the roots of negative numbers and pursued their mysterious properties. Thomas Harriot (1560-1621) was an English mathematician who was much admired by his contemporaries; he helped prepare the way for Newton. His work remains unpublished, but correspondence with his peers indicates that he studied equations with imaginary roots and it seems probable that he encountered complex numbers of the form: a+ib. However, it remained for Carl Friedrich Gauss to exploit their properties.

Gauss was born on April 30, 1777 in Brunswick, Germany, the son of poor peasants. His father was a harsh and ignorant man who wished to keep his son as ignorant as himself; his mother was a strong intelligent woman who wished to see her son educated and able to make the best of his gifts. Fortunately, the mother prevailed. His uncle Friederich, a weaver of renown in the community, was very intelligent, a genius in his own right. He recognized the boy's talent and promise and did what he could to encourage him. He spent time with the boy challenging his mental agility. Freidrich died early in life but not before Gauss recognized what his uncle had done for him.

There are tales that are hard to believe about the young child's precocity. He could "reckon" with numbers before he was three. He taught himself to read. He performed prodigious feats of calculation in school. As he developed as a mathematician his hallmark was rigor. He insisted on proofs for all the math he encountered. Ferdinand, the Duke of

Brunswick, took an interest in the youngster and became his mentor and benefactor. The Duke provided Gauss with an education culminating in several years at the University of Gottingden.

Gauss' overwhelming interest in math was the "higher arithmetic", the properties of numbers. This area of math is the most difficult; it is very demanding and difficult to understand. Gauss made a cornucopia of contributions in this area. He anticipated Hamilton in the discovery of non-commutative algebra, of which we will learn in connection with Dirac and the quantum mechanics of physics. However, in addition to math, he was very competent in a multiplicity of languages and in physics. His name is associated with the unit of magnetic induction which is named "the Gauss". Perhaps you have heard of "degaussing" a submarine; removing its magnetic signature so the enemy can not detect it by magnetic means. Gauss is responsible for the "normal distribution curve" known as the Gaussian Distribution and more familiarly to most of us as "the bell curve". He made great contributions to the computation of planetary orbits. In 1833 he invented the electric telegraph. He was prolific in math, physics, and practical invention. He was amazing!

Gauss married twice and had three children by each wife. Interestingly, he was a contemporary of Laplace, of whom we shall hear more later, and also of Napoleon. He was mentor of a splendid female mathematician named Sophie Germain; she went by the name of M. Lebanc to conceal her sex from Gauss and others. (The fair sex was not welcome in the scientific community of that time). There is a charming letter to her from Gauss written when he became aware of her deception.

He died in 1855 at the age of seventy-eight. Gauss has been called The Prince of Mathematics; he was a towering figure of the same rank as Archimedes and Newton. A short list of his contributions to math and science would be many pages long.

In complex numbers Gauss proved that all the roots of any algebraic equation have the form: a+ib. He established that these numbers can be located in a Cartesian-like plane.

Complex numbers were first enthusiastically greeted by the mathematical world because they provide the complete complement of roots for algebraic equations of any degree. An equation such as $x^4=16$ asks the question, "What value of x multiplied by itself four times equals 16?". 2 and-2 both answer the question, but so will 2i and-2i! There are four answers (roots) because the equation is of "degree four", i.e. the 'exponent' carried by "x^4" is 4. The biggest exponent in an equation determines its degree.

We have associated the positive and negative integers and zero with points on a straight line (Figure 10). In our Cartesian system we employ two such lines intersecting at right angles. Points in the **complex plane** are identified by complex numbers in an entirely analogous sense. In our Cartesian system we replace the y axis by an "iy" axis and the minus y axis by a minus iy axis. A complex number, which we'll identify with the letter z, is written: z=x+iy. For example if z=3+i7; the point z in the plane lies above x=3 and directly to the right of iy=7. In our familiar notation z has the coordinates (3,i7). z=3+i2 and z=-1-i3 are shown in Figure 17.

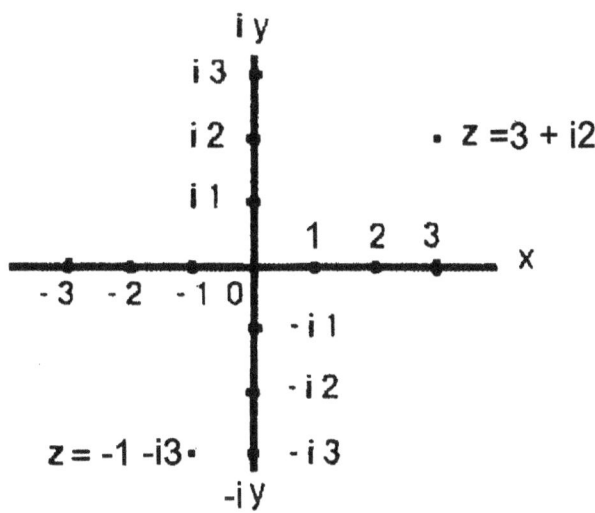

Figure 17

Complex numbers obey all the customary rules of arithmetic. i is the square root of-1 and it joins the positive and negative integers and zero in our number system. Regrettably, i is called an "imaginary" number. When it was first discovered its properties were so unusual that mathematicians of the time could not imagine that it was, in fact, a number! There is nothing imaginary about it. Like the other numbers, i represents a very precise idea, namely that (i) x (i)=-1; apart from this specialized property it obeys all the rules of arithmetic just like any other number.

To illustrate a curious property of complex numbers we recall that 5 is a prime number; it cannot be factored. At least, it can not be factored with real numbers. But (1+2i)(1-2i)=1+2i-2i-4ii=1+4=5.[*] So the prime number 5 can be factored with complex numbers! Very strange! Are we sure we know what a prime number is? Very unsettling! Why can this prime number be factored with complex numbers? Is there a message here?

This discussion of complex numbers completes our limited excursion into the realm of different kinds of numbers. To go farther we should have to walk through a door marked: Mathematicians Only. We began with the natural numbers, then the discovery of zero, then negative numbers, rational numbers, real numbers, irrational numbers, imaginary numbers, geometry, analytic geometry and complex numbers! What began with a row of beans or pebbles that had a one-to-one correspondence with a multiplicity of items grew into tallying using notches on a stick or knots on a string. Then someone discovered numbers and the items were first numbered and then counted. The number system that was born of these events has expanded into an exotic and mysterious world of abstract concepts.

---

*The multiplication in usual format is set forth below:

$$1 + 2i$$
$$\underline{1-2i}$$
$$1+2i$$
$$\underline{\ -2i-4ii}$$
$$1 +0 +4$$

(Remember (i)x(i) =-1 and-4 x-1= +4).

These are the basic tools with which we understand and control nature, but they are not natural tools,

Where do these mathematical tools come from and why do we have them? Why does a set of symbols that identifies a sequence of beans have such elaborate, useful and mysterious properties?

Now we shall look first at the calculus and then at the application of some of these powerful tools to help us understand the world about us and to uncover some very startling mysteries hidden in that world.

Chapter Eight

The Calculus

It has been said of the calculus that it is the most powerful tool known to man to enable the understanding of the world about him!

Analytic Geometry was a spark that ignited a firestorm of progress in the development of the mathematical tools needed to understand the world about us, and its natural laws; the most important of those tools is the calculus. If we are to search for clues about the Creator in the world of nature, it will be the tools associated with the calculus that will enable us to find them.

The first step toward mastering this powerful tool was to solve the problem of finding the tangent line to a curve. Why would anyone want to find the tangent line to some point on a curve? Because the slope of the tangent line is identical to the slope of the curve at that point. The "slope" of the curve is a mathematical term, At any point on the curve the slope gives the rate at which y is changing with respect to x at that point.

Well, so who cares? For one, engineers care. Let's suppose you are an engineer designing a machine that has a small piston that must move in a complicated reciprocating motion. In order to design the part so it is strong enough to experience the motion without flying apart, you need to know the forces and stresses that the part will experience at every point of its motion. In order to calculate the forces and stresses you need to know the mass of the piston and the acceleration that the piston experiences at each point in its cyclic motion. You can write an equation for the position/time history of the piston knowing the geometry of the mechanism. You then find the acceleration using the calculus (analytic geometry) and the knowledge that the slope of the position/time curve gives you the velocity, and the slope of the velocity/time curve gives you the acceleration. In this example the velocity and acceleration are **Rates**! Velocity is the rate of change of distance with time and acceleration is the rate of change of velocity with time. Rates are the "raison d'être" of the differential calculus; differential calculus *is* the calculation of rates. Finding the tangent line to a curve gives us the rate associated with the curve at that point.

We owe the first solution to this problem to a man who has been described as the greatest mathematician of the seventeenth century, Pierre Fermat. Mathematics was Fermat's hobby, he was an amateur! He lived from 1601 until 1665; consequently, he was a contemporary of Descartes and young Isaac Newton. He was born in Beaumont de Lomagne, France, the son of a leather merchant. Little is known about his youthful years or the nature of his education. He married at the age of thirty and had three sons and two daughters. As a territorial official of the French government he was a businessman. But he was more than that; he was a scholar and a brilliant mathematician. He was competent in Latin, Greek, and Spanish; he composed verse in all three languages. He lived a dignified, quiet and unassuming life. Mathematics was his recreation!

Fermat found the tangent lines to curves by a process that is very similar to what we shall encounter in the next few paragraphs. There exists a letter from Newton in which he acknowledges that he was led to the differential calculus by Fermat's method of tangents.

Fermat's first love was "the higher arithmetic", exploring the properties of numbers. He may be best-known to the public as the father of Fermat's Last Theorem. Remember the Pythagorean theorem in algebraic form: $a^2 + b^2 = c^2$? Fermat's Last Theorem states that $a^n + b^n = c^n$ has no solution for n greater than two where a, b, c, and n are all integers. Many of the most powerful minds of the last three centuries have attempted to prove the Theorem. It is only in the last decade that a mathematician named Andrew Wiles, of Princeton University accomplished the feat with eight years of effort and a very advanced set of complicated and sophisticated mathematics. Wiles' triumph received a lot of coverage in the popular newsmedia. Fermat left a note saying that he had proved it, but the margin of the book in which he wished to record it was too small to contain the proof. Did he really prove it? We shall never know!

The foregoing discussion of Analytic Geometry emphasized that the problem of the differential calculus was the problem of determining rates, and that the solution to the problem of determining rates was finding the tangent line to a curve. First, what is a tangent line? The word tangent comes from the Greek (weren't those Greeks busy inventing words?). It is a word for "touching". The tangent line to a curve is a straight line which just touches the curve at one point in such a way that it is parallel to a tiny section of the curve at the point of contact. See Figure 12 again.

When we discussed approximations, we discussed the problem of finding the exact value for the area of a circle, and we learned that this problem was solved by a procedure of successive approximations in which the circle was inscribed in one polygon and another polygon was inscribed in the circle. As the number of sides of the polygons increased toward infinity, *in the limit* the areas of the polygons were identical with the area of the circle. See Fig. 6. Finding the tangent to a curve involves the same concept of successive approximations which, *in the limit*, arrive at the exact tangent line at any point of the curve.

Let us examine the procedure which finds the tangent to any point of a continuous curve (continuous means smooth, no breaks or sharp, discontinuous changes in direction). A tangent line is a straight line that touches a continuous curve at a single point in such a way that the angle between the line and the curve is *very nearly* the same at *very* tiny distances from the point on each side. See Figure 18.

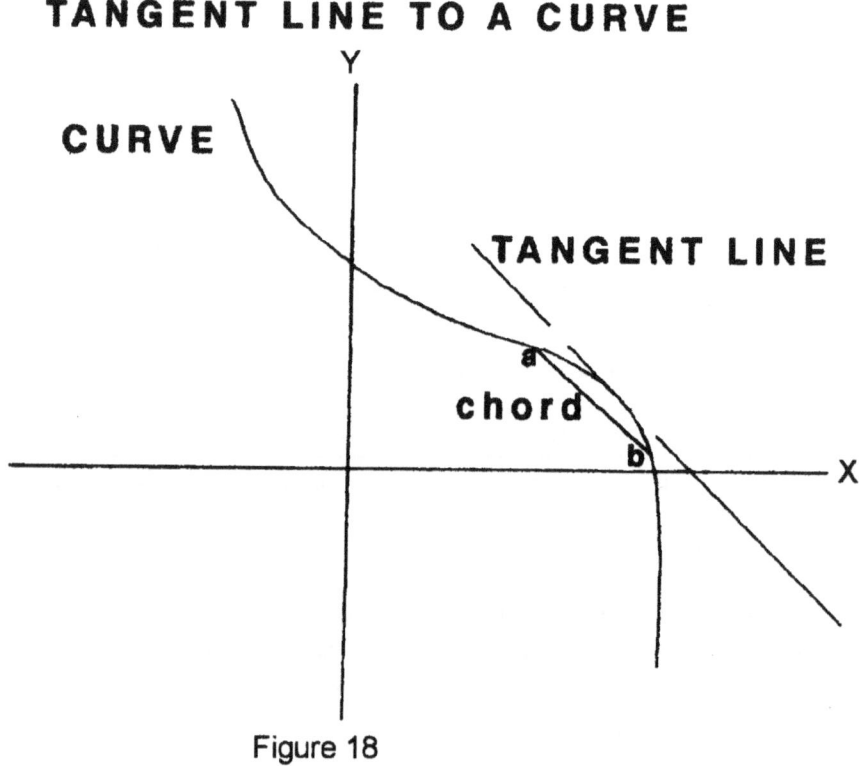

Figure 18

Figure 18 shows a chord, a straight-line segment, connecting two points a and b of the curve on either side of the tangent point. This chord is *almost* but not quite parallel to the tangent line. As the two points a and b draw closer and closer to the tangent point, the chord will become more and more nearly parallel to the tangent line. *In the limit*, when the two points a and b coincide with the tangent point, the infinitesimal chord will coincide with the tangent line.

The differential calculus finds the algebraic equation for the tangent line by a mathematical process which performs "analytically" (from whence 'analytic geometry') the same kind of limiting process we have just described.

A similar limiting process is used in the integral calculus to find the area of any plane figure. First the area is completely filled with a large number of rectangles, narrow dimension in the x direction, all rectangles parallel to each other and to the y axis. The long dimension of the rectangles is bounded by the upper and lower bounds of the area of the figure; so that the area of the figure is approximated by the total area of the enclosed rectangles. The total area of the rectangles is obtained by adding the areas of each. Then the number of rectangles is permitted to grow without limit until the area of the rectangles coincides with the area of the plane figure. This process is performed analytically by the integral calculus. See Figure 19.

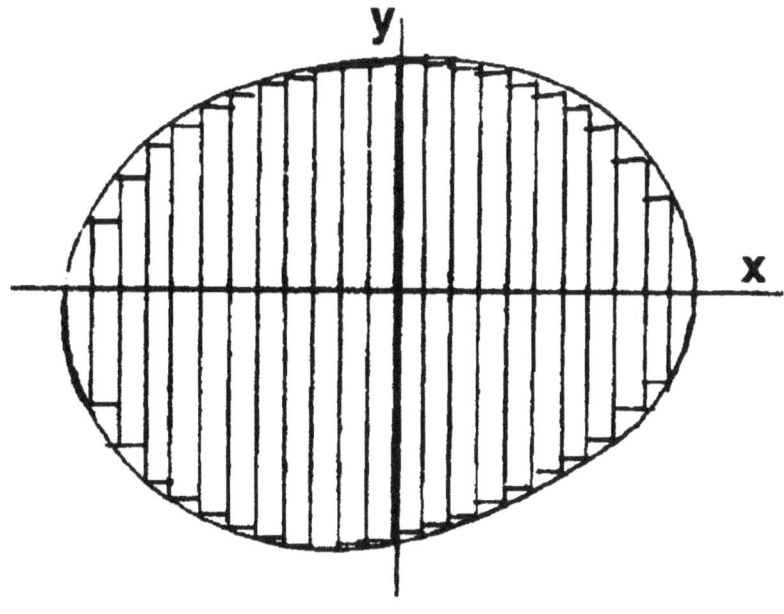

FIGURE 19

These two limiting processes of the differential and integral calculus permit mathematicians to find areas of figures and tangents to curves *exactly*! This is the monumental advance provided by the calculus.

Calculus and analytic geometry introduced an entirely new dimension to mathematics; the new dimension is *continuous* as distinguished from *discrete*. Numbers have a granularity about them, there is one unit separating any two adjacent numbers; for example, 7,456 and 7,457 are separated by one unit. The concept of infinitesimal differences, differences which may be made as small as we choose, differences which in the limit may be made zero, eliminates the granularity associated with numbers. This granularity is, of course, associated with the basic concept of a one-to-one correspondence between a row of beans and a row of other objects, the origin of the number system. A departure from this granular "row of beans" concept marked an enormous leap forward in mathematics.

Newton and Leibniz

Those who write of the brilliant mathematicians and natural philosophers who inhabited the planet in the years beginning with the fifteenth century have little to say about the spark that ignited their consuming interest in the mysteries of math and the natural world. Perhaps these remarkable individuals did not know themselves where the spark came from. Their gifts to all of us as a consequence of this consuming interest are immeasurable. In the two years 1665-1666 Newton discovered the calculus, the laws of gravitation and the nature of the composition of white light! Not until age twenty-six did Leibniz discover an interest in mathematics; then he discovered the calculus, independently of Newton, as well as the mathematics of Combinatorial Analysis! What happened to these two men to initiate these monumental discoveries? How did it happen? It is a great mystery! One wonders if—?

.

On Christmas Day, 1642, Isaac Newton was born in Woolsthorpe, England, to parents who were reasonably well-to-do farmers; he was a tiny premature baby who was not expected to survive. At the age of three his mother, who had been widowed before Isaac's birth, and who had little interest in Isaac, left him to the care of his grandmother and married a Mr. Smith. Isaac was somewhat frail as a child, and he amused himself with the construction of mechanical toys and extensive reading. When Isaac was fifteen, Mr. Smith perished and Isaac's mother returned to the village of his birth. Although he was clearly precocious, he did not exhibit any unusual powers as a child or teen. However, an uncle recognized something exceptional in the boy and was responsible for convincing his mother that he should go to the university at Cambridge rather than help her manage the farm. As a student at Trinity College, Cambridge, Newton had the good fortune to have a Dr. Isaac Barrow as teacher of mathematics and mentor. Dr. Barrow's lectures on such things as finding the tangent to a curve probably guided Newton toward the discovery of the calculus.

In 1664 the University was closed for two years, a result of the Great Plague, and Newton retired to the family farm; there he discovered "the method of fluxions", the predecessor of today's calculus. While he was there, and in his early twenties, he also made two other remarkable discoveries. The first is the law of gravitation, namely that every body in the universe is attracted to every other body by a force which is proportional to the product of their masses and inversely proportional to the square of the distance between them; the second is that white light is composed of light of all colors!

After the bubonic plague receded, he returned to Cambridge. In 1669 Dr. Barrow, who recognized the great promise of his student, resigned the Lucasian Professorship of Mathematics in favor of Newton. The Lucasian chair is presently occupied by the famous physicist and cosmologist Stephen Hawkings, author of a recent popular book, "A Brief History of Time". The Lucasian Chair has a history of stellar occupants. The first star, and the most brilliant, was Newton. Apart from Einstein, author of the theories of Special and General Relativity and an explanation of the photoelectric effect, it is difficult to find a mind equal to that of Newton. He collected his work in a huge book written in Latin (the language of science in his day): Philosophiae Naturalis Principia Mathematica (1687). His "Principia" dominated much of science and mathematics for all of the 18th century.

Newton died at age eighty-five in 1727; he may have had the finest mathematical mind in history; he was a giant. But he had this to say about himself, "I do not know what I may appear to the world, but to myself I seem to have been only like a boy playing on the seashore and diverting myself in now and then finding a smoother pebble or a prettier shell than ordinary; whilst the great ocean of truth lay all undiscovered before me". He is buried in Westminster Abbey.

Gottfried Wilhelm Leibniz was born into a good family at Leipzig in 1646. His father was a professor of philosophy. At age fifteen Gottfried entered the University of Leipzig as a law student. He was active in the law until the age of twenty-six when he met Christian Huygens, a mathematician and physicist, in Paris. Huygens agreed to teach Leibniz mathematics and for a time Leibniz devoted all his energies to math. He made many contributions to calculus and combinatorial analysis. Later he turned to politics and diplomacy and devoted the balance of his life to those pursuits. It is a great pity that his powerful mind was so poorly occupied. He died in 1716.

The calculus was born in the seventeenth century to two fathers, Isaac Newton and Gottfried Leibniz. It was the brilliant Leibniz who developed the notation, still used today, that made it tractable. Leibniz also laid the foundation for symbolic reasoning, which is based on the discrete as distinct from the continuous! This foundation is called "Combinatorial Analysis". Combinatorial Analysis includes not only symbolic logic in its domain but also the theory of probability. Combinatorial analysis begins with "permutations and combinations"; a subject which is probably remembered with horror by those who encountered it in highschool. As a reminder to those who have blocks, "permutation" involves the study of the order in which a multiplicity of items can be arranged. A simple example: in how many ways can we order the letters a,b,c? (abc, acb, cab, cba, bac, bca; six ways). "Combinations" involves the study of the number of sets into which a group of individual items (letters for example) can be grouped; "m things taken n at a time", ten letters taken two at a time can form how many sets? This answer is left to the reader. The body of logic that devolves from these kinds of studies is the foundation for studies of the distribution of objects into classes.

The mathematics of the discrete is fundamental to the quantum mechanics and other modern sciences. In fact, it is so fundamental that we jump ahead to the beginning of the twentieth century to note that it is Max Planck and Albert Einstein to whom we owe the discoveries of the quantum of energy. The fact that matter and energy are "quantized", i.e.granular, are discoveries shared by Planck and Einstein. Both men were Nobel Laureats. The two brilliant men were friends who had great respect for each other and also a mutual love for music. They were both accomplished musicians and played together. Their discoveries in the years between 1900 and 1905 revolutionized physics and man's understanding of the natural world! The granular nature of nature made the discrete mathematics of Leibniz the foundation of modern quantum theories.

Newton's exposition of the method of fluxions (the calculus) used a notation that was difficult to grasp. On the Continent, Leibniz had discovered many of the properties of the calculus independently of, but later than, Newton. He was ignorant of Newton's achievements because Newton had a secretive nature and had not published his findings. Leibniz invented a greatly improved notation for the calculus and was being recognized on the Continent, in 1693, as the discoverer of the method. At this point Leibniz and Newton enjoyed a courteous and cordial relationship, but subsequently the issue of priority of discovery was taken up on a national scale! As a result of French and English national hubris, and encouraged by nationalist comrades, the former

friends engaged in a scurrilous argument over who had been the origi-
nator of the calculus. It seems clear that it was Newton, and it is a blot
on his record that he participated in this shabby debate.

What kind of men were Newton and Leibniz? Did they share their
marvelous discovery with amity and graciousness? Were they the Damon
and Pythias of the seventeenth century? No, in the end, they were trucu-
lent, jealous competitors.

Although the calculus is a child attributed to Newton and Leibniz there
is evidence that the limiting processes on which it is founded were known
to Archimedes and to Fermat. In fact, it is at least fair to say that the seeds
were planted by the latter two men, and the harvest was reaped by
Newton and Leibniz.

The seed from Archimedes in the third century BC did not germinate
and flower until the seventeenth century, 2000 years later. Why was there
this enormous 2000 year gap between the time of Archimedes, who was
aware of the kernels of the ideas on which the calculus is based, and its cul-
mination with Newton and Leibniz? The delay in the discovery of this
astounding gift is extremely curious. Might we suspect intervention? Did
some careful hand decide that Homo sapiens should mature a bit more
before being awarded this powerful tool? Or is it just an accident of history? What do you think?

Chapter Nine

Analysis and Reason
are Established

If a benign Creator is at work in our world, then surely he was instrumental in replacing dogma, bigotry and superstition with logic and reason. What were the intellectual factors that account for this monumental change? Mathematics and experimentation were the keys.

Before Reason could prevail, relating cause to effect in a quantitative sense had to replace conjecture and superstition in the understanding of natural phenomena. Understanding natural phenomena required: first, experimentation, second, construction of theories that would account for the experimental results and third, a mathematical basis for those theories which would yield quantitative confirmation of experimental measurements. This procedure required a broad spectrum of mathematical tools.

The basic mathematical tools needed for these tasks are: the numbers, the geometry, analytic geometry, combinatorial analysis, and the calculus. Newton and Leibniz put the last of these basic tools in the "natural philosopher's" tool-box. With these tools a succession of brilliant physicists and mathematicians, "natural philosophers" in the argot of the 19th century, discovered the rules, the "natural laws", governing the behavior of light, atoms, heat, fluid flow, celestial mechanics and special and general relativity, all this in the space of 300 years!

As the "natural philosophers" appeared and began to study the physical world and to try to predict in quantitative terms the behavior of common objects: the behavior of a ball rolling down an incline, the behavior of falling bodies (let's be grateful for Galileo and the Leaning Tower of Pisa), the motion of a pendulum, the motion of the planets in the heavens, the behavior of light and sound, etc., mathematical tools were often available to support the analysis. When the tools were not at hand the analyst often invented (or discovered) the math he needed to proceed.

Many powerful and beautiful mathematical tools were added and continue to be added to the tool-box. Today's scientist, with the present contents of the tool-box and the computational power of digital computers, can attack just about any problem of which the human mind can conceive. **But he can not account for his ability to express the natural laws in mathematical terms. Neither can he account for the Cause behind the natural laws.** *The Eternal Mystery remains a total mystery.*

The River

The 17th and 18th centuries saw many tools added to the scientists' and mathematicians' tool boxes. The trickle of scientific and mathematical knowledge, which began with Pythagorus and Archimedes, became a stream as Fermat, Newton, Leibniz, Galileo and other brilliant scholars of that time poured their contributions into it. The stream of knowledge that began as a trickle, because there was no readily available means to exchange and disseminate information, swelled to a river, a river which flowed freely in a communication channel provided by the written and printed word.

Writing materials were difficult to come by at the time the Egyptians and Babylonians were developing an ability to make mathematical computations. Clay tablets were awkward and cumbersome; papyrus was fragile and somewhat loathe to take ink. Reproductions were made by scribes who copied by hand with the inevitable incursion of errors. There were signet stones, first in Babylonia, which were the first tools to incorporate offset printing. Later, the Greeks, Egyptians and Romans made extensive use of squads of slaves to hand-copy books. This created another problem since the slaves had to be literate! Monks in monasteries spent lifetimes creating beautiful illuminated manuscripts. Books there were, in those days, but they were available to only a privileged few, and were often devoted to religious, not scientific or mathematical, subjects.

Meanwhile, in far-away China, paper was invented about 100 AD This was a watershed event, for paper is rugged and readily accepts ink. The Chinese used wood-block offset techniques to print on their new invention, but their picto-character words were not well adapted to voluminous libraries. Just before the turn of the first millenium the Chinese also tried moveable type, but found the whole thing too complex. Fortunately, paper found its way to the West and was available in Europe when Johann Gutenberg needed it.

Johann Gutenberg is credited with the first use of moveable metal type in 1450. It is believed that he was born just before the beginning of the 15th century in Mainz, Germany. Little is known of his life. He was trained as a goldsmith, but he became interested in printing and conducted experiments in that art as a young man. He later formed a partnership with a Johann Fust to whom he later lost his business as the result of a lawsuit. Gutenberg's success with moveable type was the consequence of an invention: moveable metal type characters were cast with such precision that they could be confined in a tray by edge constraints, without falling out. He died February 3, 1468 in Mainz.

Martin Luther and the Reformation created a market for Gutenberg's invention; the religious rebellion demanded the printing of pamphlets and other documents expounding the new philosophy. The pamphlets and documents poured gasoline on a fiery conflict among different religious factions. By mid 1600 printing was to be found everywhere in the Western World, one page per pressing. Printing at this time was an enormous advance, but it was a slow and laborious process. Then in 1871 Richard Hoe perfected printing from rolls of paper rather than from sheets. Shortly thereafter there was a rapid progression of the typesetting art: manual typesetting gave way to mechanical typesetting. This was followed by phototypesetting, which was followed by computers. Computers set type, incorporate photos and artwork, and then coalesce all these onto a single sheet of film or a printing plate.

The twentieth century marked the ready availability of books, magazines, newspapers and other versions of the printed word. Bookstores and libraries were to be found everywhere in the Western World; the River of Knowledge was now a torrent carried forward by paper and ink. How could this marvel of information flow be improved?

By the Internet, of course! Still in its infancy as the twenty-first century dawns, the Internet has already caused the River to overflow its banks! In any third-world country a gasoline powered generator, a satellite dish and a computer provide access to all the information in the world! The River flows over a riverbed of science and mathematics; without these two there would be no river. What is the purpose of that River? Why do we have it? As we follow the River where will it lead us?

Mathematical Consistency in Nature

It is an astounding fact that many unrelated natural processes are described by the same mathematical equations. Wave motion is perhaps the most obvious example. Star light, sound, the motion of vibrating strings, vibrating membranes, electric waves on transmission lines, optical waves in tiny optical fibers, vibrations in organ pipes, waves in fluids, waves in solids, all these resonate to the same kind of mathematics. We shall look at a few instances of this remarkable property of our universe, this mathematical consistency in nature, and wonder at the good fortune we enjoy because of this fact. Did some benign hand program a cooperative physical world and then provide us with brains which could acquire the mathematical skills with which we could learn about and control that world? Or is it just a coincidence? We wonder—.We shall begin with exponential processes for they are at work everywhere in nature.

Nature's Growth Rate

As we look at nature through the eyes of math and science we shall continue to wonder at the way in which one mathematical equation will apply to a multitude of unrelated phenomena. As an example we shall consider Nature's Growth Rate; it applies to phenomena as unrelated as bacteria, bank accounts and electrical currents! All these phenomena are characterized by the concept that the growth of a quantity is related to the amount of the quantity present. Clearly, the architect of natural processes was fond of this one. Mathematicians call these "exponential processes".

Let's turn to a very physical phenomenon that will illustrate exponential growth. Let's talk about **rabbits!** Now, if someone says to you that, starting with one pair of rabbits in the garage, a male and a female of course, as time progresses (at a constant rate, of course, which is what time does) the rate of increase in the rabbit population will be proportional to the number of rabbits in the garage; you will probably agree with that equation. The greater the number of rabbits, the greater the number of baby rabbits. Soon there is a population explosion and we are inundated with rabbits!.The same equation will apply to a population of fruitflies in a jar, bacteria in a petrie dish, and so on.

The simple equation which describes the growth of the rabbit population, making the assumption that the growth is continuous, is:

$$R = R_0\, e^{kt}$$

where R is the size of the population at time "t", k is just a constant number, kt is an exponent (for an explanation of exponents see Appendix Two) which is associated with the base "e", and R_0 is the size of the population at the time t=0 (i.e. two rabbits in our example). The letter "e" is a symbol for the "natural base". See Appendix One for more about this equation.

The "natural base 'e'" occurs in the time-history of many natural processes. The base of the number system we all use in our daily lives is ten (10). Now, ten is just a number word and 10 is the symbol we use to designate the number word "ten". "e" is both a number word and a symbol, it designates the number 2.718281828459045.... Here the dots mean the decimal number never ends! But, "e" is still just a number like ten. 10^2 = 100; e^2 = 7.389...No mystery, two different numbers multiplied by themselves give two different answers. But "e" has some very special and mysterious properties as we shall see shortly.

Bankers want an exact formula for money growth, one that deals with the continuous. Bankers want the formula in order to calculate (continuously) compounded interest. The interest being earned at any time is proportional to the size of the principal in the account. This interest is added continuously to the principal, i.e. the interest is compounded. The account grows exponentially. (You have undoubtedly heard the stories to the effect that if the Meddicis had put there wealth at compound interest in the sixteenth century they would now own all the money in the world. Exponential growth is powerful!)

The same equation that describes rabbit growth describes money growth over time when interest is compounded. Since most of us are closer to money than to rabbits, let's choose an interest bearing savings account for an example. To begin, let's rewrite the equation in terms of Principal (P), annual interest rate (k), and the time in years (t). When we make the initial deposit to the bank we deposit P_0 dollars on January first which is time t = 0.

$$P = P_0 \, e^{kt}$$

Look familiar? Of course! There are tables that list the values of e^n where n is some integer or decimal number. Once we know k and t we can multiply them together and look up the corresponding number for e^{kt}. Let's calculate the size of our bank account for t = 1, 10, and 100 years with k = 5% interest rate compounded. We'll start with a $10,000 deposit, i.e. P_0 = $10,000. To calculate our principal at the end of year one we look up kt = 0.05x1 = 0.05 in the table listing values of e^n and discover that $e^{0.05}$ = 1.051. At the end of year one we will have $10,000 times 1.051 or $10,510. For year 10 we look up 0.05x10 = 0.5 and find we will have $16,490; and for year 100 we look up 0.05x100 = 5 and discover we will have $1,484,000. With straight (not compounded) 5% interest on our $10,000 principal we would have only $60,000 at the end of 100 years. If we keep the product kt the same, multiplying k by 4 (20% interest) and divide the time t by four (25 years), we learn that 20% interest yields the same $1,484,000 in 25 years.

Young people with a $10,000 initial investment that earns 20% interest, compounded, in the stock market can retire with a tidy sum in 25 years. That is, *if* the stock market continues to yield 20% over those twenty-five years! Compound interest is very powerful!

Let's return to the garage and find out what the rabbits are doing. (We know what they're doing!) The rabbit population is increasing at an *exponential* rate; that means that if the population is 2 (to start with), then soon, very soon, there are rabbits everywhere!

Let's see how this works (for the sake of illustration let's accelerate the gestation period for rabbits). Let's suppose that every week the number of rabbits doubles; 2, 4, 8, 16, 32, 64, 128, 256, 512, 1024,... when they double during equal time intervals they are increasing at an exponential rate! If it was a linear rate, where the increase is the same in each time interval, the numbers would be 2,4,6,8,10,12,14..., a very slow rate by comparison with an exponential rate. This would be the result if the first pair continued to reproduce but all of their children were sterile. But their children are far from sterile! At the end of nine weeks there are over 1000 rabbits, at the end of 18 weeks there are over a million! The same sequence of numbers applies to our individual human histories. If we think in terms of human lineage, we have two parents, four grandparents, eight great grandparents,…, the same as a rabbit! One million ancestors in about 400 years! This is very convenient for family genealogists, because they can select for study and bragging rights the cream of the crop. Like all of the Irish, we are each descended from Kings and Nobles!

But this forecast of rabbit population is only an *approximation*, because there is a weekly granularity (remember discrete) to the increase in rabbits; it is not continuous. As we all know, the entire group of rabbits doesn't wait until Monday night to do it! If the rabbit population is very, very large our best approximation to their population growth will be based on a continuous rather than a discrete model. The equation with which we began this discussion provides a solution for the continuous model. To learn more about this equation see Appendix One.

Exponential processes are at work everywhere in nature, in both the biological world and the world of physics. In the world of physics we see exponential growth and decay of transient currents in electrical circuits. When you turn on your TV voltages are applied, currents and electrical charges are set into motion and they quickly stabilize after having experienced a growth which follows a mathematics which is analogous to our "rabbit equation". When you turn your TV off the currents and charges decay following the same mathematics. See Appendix One. This behavior is true not only of electrical circuits but also of all linear physical systems. It is amazing that so much of biological and physical nature follows the dictates of exponential mathematics.

Chapter Ten

The Amazing "e" and Its Cousin "pi"

There is a close and remarkable relationship between e and pi; for both are intimately associated with a circle, as we shall see when we meet Euler's Famous Formula. Yet, both e and pi are just numbers, e = 2.718…and pi = 3.141…Now think about that for a moment: rabbits, circles, compound interest, transients in electrical circuits and some more remarkable relationships; all are associated with these two very special numbers. This commonality among very diverse physical processes, mathematics and geometrical figures is astounding! What kind of clues lurk beneath the utility that these numbers provide to scientists and business operations? *Are we to accept these kinds of strange mysteries without probing for deeper answers?*

As we know, there is a number that multiplied by itself fits the natural growth of rabbits, bacteria, bank accounts etc. This number is 2.7182818…; it is designated by mathematicians as "e". It is called "the natural base" for obvious reasons; in natural processes there is a predisposition for the base to be "e". When the base is "e" and the time is regular clock time the actual growth of bacteria populations and bank accounts fits the numbers calculated using "e" as the base. Like pi, e is a decimal number with an infinite number of digits. To learn more about "e" and how it is calculated see Appendix Three.

But quite apart from its relationship to rabbits and compound interest and other natural phenomena e has some mysterious and wonderful purely mathematical properties, and its *discovery* has engaged many of the great mathematicians of the nineteenth and twentieth centuries in the task of exploring all of its properties. One of these mathematicians was named Leonard Euler.

Euler's Famous Formula

In the next few paragraphs we will encounter a very, very curious and important mathematical formula.

Why is this formula important to us? It is important to us because, like Russia, it is a "puzzle wrapped in an enigma". It illustrates the "other worldly" properties of mathematics.

When confronted with this formula in the 19th century, Harvard's Benjamin Pierce, a renowned mathematician, is said to have observed to his class, "Gentlemen, that formula is surely true, it is absolutely paradoxical; we can not understand it, and we don't know what it means, but we have proved it and therefore, we know it must be the truth." So if the reader is a bit mystified by what follows he or she is in good company!

Using a relationship discovered by DeMoivre, (See Appendix 4) Leonard Euler developed the following remarkable formula:

$$e^{(pi \times i)} = -1$$

This formula has been called, "The most famous and compact of all formulas". Euler found it so beautiful and unique that he had it put above the gate of the Academy in Saint Petersburg, Russia.

Now let's write out the above equation, $e^{(pi \times i)} = -1$, using numbers in place of the symbols:

$(2.7182818...)^{(3.14...\times (-1)^{1/2}} = -1$ (i is written as $(-1)^{1/2}$).

How can that be? It makes no sense! And why does that menagerie of numbers equal an inconsequential-1?

Study the term on the left side of the equals sign. The square root of-1, $(-1)^{1/2}$), is not a natural number; neither are the two numbers 2.7182818…and 3.14…with their infinite quantities of digits! There is no way to evaluate this complex term numerically! Yet we *know* it equals -1. Now is that a strange discovery or what? **Does this riddle give us a glimpse into the mind of the Creator?**

The foregoing material is not easy to understand, or, better said, is not understandable, as witness Professor Pierce's comment to his class. So don't try to understand it; you will fail as everyone does.

Adventuresome readers will want to turn to Appendix Three, study the figures drawn to illustrate the text, and review the material two or three times if necessary. When you have assimilated this material you will be rewarded with a glimpse into a world that is usually reserved for mathematicians and physicists; it is a very strange world, most intriguing and wonderful, and well-worth the effort needed to peek into it!

Leonard Euler was born in Basel, Switzerland on April 15, 1707 to a Calvinist minister and his wife. Young Leonard displayed both an interest and an ability in mathematics, but his father insisted that his life's work should be in theology. Fortunately, he was rescued by one of the Bernoullis (a famous family of accomplished mathematicians) who convinced Leonard's father that he was destined to be a great mathematician. Thus began a distinguished and prolific mathematical career. At this time, early in the 18th century, there were two famous and productive centers of scientific study, one in St. Petersburg, Russia and one in Berlin, Germany. Euler found his way first to St. Petersburg, married, and spent thirteen years of intense work there with his mathematics, then in 1740 he moved to Berlin where he was supported by Frederick the Great. In 1766 it was back to St. Petersburg at the invitation of Catherine the Great. Having lost the sight of one eye some years before, he now began to lose the sight of the other and became totally blind. Blindness did not decrease his productivity! He was possessed of a marvelous memory and the ability to do complex calculations in his head. He died in 1783 at age 77. He left behind an enormous legacy of discoveries and mathematical papers

Let's pause for a bit and ponder. We shall see that these *numbers*, e and pi and the imaginary designator i, need not be related to nature or man except, perhaps, for man's concept of a one-to-one correspondence between a quantity of pebbles and a like quantity of objects. That is to say, there must be a number system before these quantities, expressed as numbers, have meaning. Once there is the concept of a number system, e, pi, and i can be dealt with as numbers independent of any physical objects. Indeed pi can be expressed independently of geometrical considerations by the following infinite series:

$$pi = 4(1-1/3+1/5-1/7+1/9-1/11+1/13-....)$$

so there is no need for the concept of a circle and its diameter in establishing a *number* equal to pi; and

$$e= 1 + 1 + 1/2 + 1/6 + 1/24 + 1/120 +....$$

independent of nature, rabbits, or compound interest. These are just numbers. Although both are *also* associated with a geometric figure, a circle, they are, when defined as the sum of an infinite series, just numbers. They have, as numbers, no real relationship to anything in nature; they can exist on an intellectual level as solely intellectual entities!

Before we leave this discussion let's take a second look. Part of the equation for pi, i.e. the series in parentheses, is made up of *all* the odd integers and *only* the odd integers. This numerical sum is one quarter of pi, one quarter of the ratio of the circumference of a circle to its diameter, a geometrical quantity. Now is that strange or what? *Why do all the odd integers, and only the odd integers, relate to one quarter of the ratio of a circle's circumference to its diameter?*

e, the sum of another series of numbers, appears in nature (rabbits) and finance when the rate of increase of a quantity is proportional to the amount of the quantity present; however, it can be defined by a series of numbers, independent of anything else. Yet there is also a geometric relationship between e and the circle through the DeMoivre equation. Through this relationship we know that e raised to the (pi)(i) power equals -1, in other words **is** -1! Now -1 is really an invention (or discovery) of man, not a number which can be associated with a pebble, an object; nor can i be associated with a pebble, it is the square root of -1. Pi is a *ratio* of object dimensions, the ratio of the circumference of a circle to its diameter, so it can not be associated with a pebble, an object. Likewise e is a never-ending decimal number, it can not be associated with a pebble. What are we to make of this strange relationship among quantities which are expressible in terms of natural numbers but are not, in that sense, numbers at all?

"Pi and e are, after all, only numbers". Is that statement really correct? No, both e and pi are more than only numbers; they are also important inhabitants of the natural world. They have a dual nature. As we shall see later in this book, light waves, electrons, and every speck of matter also have a dual nature, they are each both particles and waves! The parallel nature of particles and waves on the one hand and numbers and nature on the other is most intriguing! After a few moments thought it seems very unlikely that there is no coupling between these curiosities. Should we be looking for a clue in this parallelism? **Is there an insight to the Creator's nature in this disturbing parallel?**

In addition to the uncomfortable wave-particle duality, nature has been created in such a way that it contains other features, mysteries, which contradict our everyday experience. Should a ten-pound lead ball fall to the ground faster than a one-pound lead ball? Of course it should! That's what everyone **knew** until Galileo climbed the Leaning Tower of Pisa and dropped the weights! It was Newton who explained that the larger force associated with the heavier weight was offset by its larger mass; so both light objects and heavy objects would experience the same acceleration as they fell to earth. In a similar way, the smaller weight of a motorcycle can be accelerated equally with the greater weight of a large automobile if the force delivered by each of the two motors is proportional to the mass of its vehicle. The motors overcome the inertia of the two vehicles. (Inertia is the property of a body that causes it to continue at rest or at a constant speed in the same direction in the absence of an external force).

Everyone **knew** the earth was the center of the universe in the centuries following the birth of Christ; it was Copernicus who rectified that cosmic error. Everyone **knew** that the flow of time was invariant until Einstein's theory of Relativity proved otherwise. There have been many more such errors in our convictions. Newton, Copernicus, Euler and Einstein solved many mysteries of the natural world with the mysteries of mathematics; pi and the amazing e played a prominent role in these solutions.

As we have seen, pi and e inhabit not only the natural world but also the intellectual world of math; a world which is independent of nature. The idea that mathematics enjoys an existence independent of man goes back at least to Plato who, perhaps tongue-in-cheek (perhaps not), entertains the idea that mathematics is a gift of the gods. Math is eternal, there will never come a time when the discoveries that we have encountered thus far will not be true. Nothing in nature is eternal in the sense that our universe is headed for extinction. The physicists say, "The entropy of the universe is continually increasing."; that is to say that disorder is continually increasing. The ultimate fate of the universe appears to be total disorder; earth will be a dead planet in a cold dead universe. But in the midst of the death of the universe, mathematics will survive. In this sense, math is not "natural", is it? If it is not "natural", what is it? Supernatural? **Why is math the way it is?**

Now we have a pretty good idea of the basic tools in the mathematical toolbox. To be sure, there are many other tools, some with very general applications, but we have our hammer, saw, screwdriver and carpenter's square, enough to build the case we are studying. With these tools at hand let's take a look at the natural world; a very broad look that will encounter some physics and chemistry, but will go beyond in order to observe some highly improbable discoveries that have shaped the world as it is today.

Chapter Eleven

Electricity, Gravity and the Wave Equation

The remaining chapters in this book look at nature through the eyes of science. If we Homo sapiens are to catch a glimpse of the Creator's nature, it will be through knowledge of his work: the universe, our planet, ourselves and the laws he has established that govern all of these elements of our lives. Revelations about our world have come through the gifts with which certain men and women have been endowed; we shall meet some of them briefly because they were very special people. Perhaps their personalities and lives will enlighten us also.

Fundamental to all of physics are three familiar natural phenomena: electricity, gravity and waves. We shall begin our look at nature with these three. The most fundamental of the three is probably waves. As the natural world is dissected one encounters waves everywhere! Modern physics finds waves in the tiny world of quantum physics, in light and other electromagnetic phenomena, and suspects that waves are the foundation of gravity as well. Tiny packets of wave energy appear at the very limits of modern physical theory. The mathematics of electricity, gravity and waves began with a French mathematician in the 18th century.

The Equations of La Place and Poisson

Pierre Simon Laplace was born in 1749 to peasant parents in Beaumont-en-Auge, France; an humble origin of which he was ashamed all of his life. At the age of eighteen he headed for Paris, then as now, the center of the French universe. He was befriended by Jean le Rond d'Alembert who was also of humble origin having been the bastard son of a French chevalier, abandoned on the local church steps by his mother and raised in humble circumstances by a poor glazier. It is d'Alembert to whom we owe the "wave equation" which he discovered while analyzing the motion of a vibrating string and of which we shall learn more in the next section of this chapter. d'Alembert secured a position for Laplace as professor of mathematics at the Military School of Paris. Laplace made great contributions to mathematical astronomy and to the theory of probability. He devoted much of his life to a study of the solar system.

At the time in which Laplace lived there were grave concerns that the solar system might be unstable, that the sun and the planets together with their moons might be subject to an instability caused by the interaction of the mutual gravitational attraction of all these massive bodies. As a result of the instability there would be either some titanic crashes among the planets or else some members of this heavenly host would spin away into the void. Our solar system is an extremely complex system, and its analysis would intimidate any mathematical analyst. But Laplace solved the problem, albeit in a somewhat simplified form, and the solution established that the system is stable. So thanks to Pierre Simon we can sleep peacefully tonight. His studies of celestial mechanics led him into the theory of probability which he developed to a high degree of perfection. The theory of probability was first studied by Pascal and Fermat. Their initial interest in probability is said to have been stimulated by gamblers who came to Pascal for knowledge of the odds in games of chance. Probability theory is the mathematical basis for quantum mechanics, the physics of atoms and their nuclei; it occupies a stellar role not only in the casinos of Las Vegas but also in modern physics.

Perhaps Laplace's greatest contribution to mathematical physics was the concept of the potential. The discovery of this concept made possible the solution of problems which would otherwise have been nearly unsolvable. What do we mean by the word "potential" in this context? Let's choose a simple example making use of gravity, with which we are all familiar, and to which we are eternally grateful since without it we would all fly off the surface of the planet and become spacepersons.

If we carry a pound of coffee to the top of a 100 foot high hill the coffee's potential (energy) has increased by 100 foot-pounds, one pound moving 100 feet vertically against gravity. Suppose the hill is a perfect cone; we are at the north side and three of our friends each carry their pound of coffee up the hill, but each of them is at one of the other compass points: east, south, west. At each ten foot marker the potential for each of them is the same, and we picture concentric circles around the cone which are lines of "equipotential". But, you say, these are just the familiar contour lines we find on a topographical map! You are 100% right! Now you have the concept of potential, and also the important concept that the gravitational force is directed at right angles to the equipotential lines, i.e. downhill, as any skier can affirm! Physicists call this gravitational force the "potential gradient"; no doubt because balls roll downhill under the influence of gravity in the direction of the steepest grade. If we can determine the potential in a physical problem, LaPlace has made it very easy for us to find the related potential gradient using a simple procedure employing the calculus. The potential gradient of the gravitational potential is the gravitational force; the potential gradient of the electric potential is the electric force; the potential gradient of the thermal potential is oriented in the direction that heat will flow from a body at a higher temperature to a body at a lower temperature, and so on. The concept of potential is a marvelous concept of very general application in physical problems, and we owe much to M. Laplace for discovering it. It renders many difficult problems tractable.

Let's write down the formulas for gravitational and electric forces of attraction, as we shall see they are mathematically identical:

The force acting on each of two bodies under the influence of gravity is:

$$F = -kmM/d^2$$

F: force of attraction

k: a constant number
m: mass of first body
M: mass of second body
d: distance separating m & M

The force acting on each of two electrically charged bodies one +, one - is:

$$F = -kqQ/d^2$$

F: force of attraction
k: a constant number
q: charge on first body
Q: charge on second body
d: distance separating q & Q

The minus signs indicate that the two forces are forces of attraction. The form of these two equations is exactly the same! Both are examples of what is known to physicists as "Central Force" phenomena.

How remarkable that gravitational and electrical forces should have the same mathematical form! What simple and elegant solutions flow from nature as embodied in Laplace's Equation! Laplace's Equation can be solved for velocity potential, electrical potential and gravitational potential to determine the velocities in fluid flow, electric fields of force, and gravitational forces among physical bodies (heavenly and otherwise). One simple equation unites all these different segments of nature! Furthermore, Laplace's Equation can be used to determine the steady state temperatures in a bar of metal (round or square cross section) when the temperatures at the boundaries (the two ends and the cylindrical surface) are known. This is an example of a large class of problems known as "boundary value problems" which are solvable using Laplace's Equation.

Why does one simple equation apply to all these different physical phenomena? Who would expect this kind of commonality among gravity, fluid flow, heat and electricity? Who would expect that the rules, that is to say the mathematical equations, would be the same for the forces with which the sun and the planets tug at each other and the forces exerted among the tiny electrons? *How come?* Mind boggling! Very hard to believe! As Frenchman Laplace might say, "Quelle elegance"!.

Unjustifiably, Simeon-Denis Poisson is given short shrift in the literature, but "Poisson's Equation" is well-known to students of electricity and magnetism. Poisson made many other valuable contributions to probability theory, mechanics, elasticity and differential equations; it is a mystery that he appears only briefly on the historical mathematical radar screen. Poisson's Equation is an extension of Laplace's equation. Whereas Laplace's equation applies in a volume of space where there are no electrical charges, Poisson's equation applies to a volume of space that contains electrical charges. These two equations permit us to find solutions for electrostatic problems; "electrostatic" means that the electrical charges are stationary. Poisson's equation applies not only to electrical charges but also to mass points in space, heat sources, and fluid flow.

Here again we see a remarkable unity in the mathematical description of the physical world. Let's not pass it by too quickly; the unity among these diverse physical phenomena is awesome! One would simply not expect it! **One is persuaded that this unity carries the thumbprint of the Creator.**

The Wave Equation

Most of us are conscious of the multitude of different kinds of waves that surround us: sound waves, radio waves, light waves, ocean waves. It is a marvel of math and physics that we can understand and manage waves of almost every nature. It is an even greater marvel that one mathematical concept permits us to analyze these waves.

What is a wave? Picture a long ridge of water moving toward the shore. This is a wave crest that will alert every surfer in the neighborhood to start paddling toward shore so he can catch the wave. This wave crest is followed by another and another and another. The distance between wave crests is called the wave-length and the rate at which the wave crests pass a fixed point is called the frequency. If, now, instead of riding the wave we and our surfboard are stationary in the water we will bob up and down, up and down, as the waves pass. If we make a chart of our vertical position as it changes with time we will produce what mathematicians call a sinusoidal wave. (We encounter sinusoidal waves in Appendix Four in connection with Euler's Famous Formula; refer to that Appendix for more about sinusoidal waves). The sinusoidal form is very fundamental to our understanding of nature and, indeed, to the way nature behaves. It is the form taken by vibrating strings (first analyzed by d'Alembert as noted in the previous section) which are emitting a single tone; it occurs in the analysis of light and sound, and in quantum mechanics; it is very important! See Figure 20 for a graph of a sinusoidal wave.

Sinusoidal Waves

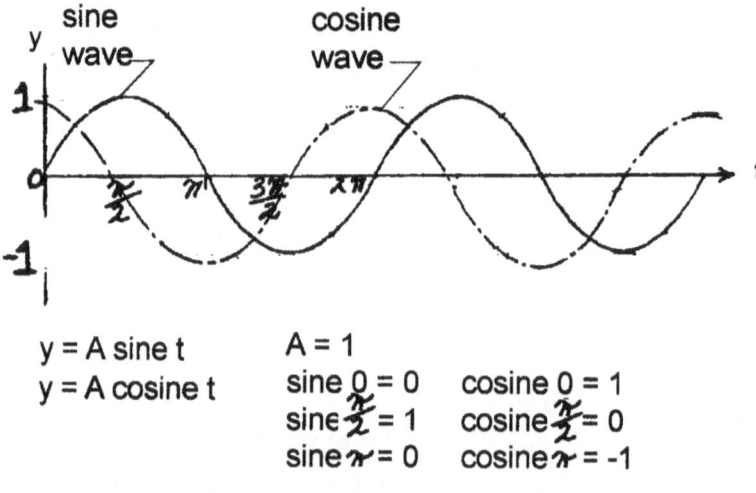

Figure 20

Why so much emphasis on waves and the wave equation? It is because waves figure so prominently in our universe: sound waves, pressure waves in solids, electric waves on power transmission lines, destructive waves in suspension bridges when high winds cause them to vibrate like d'Alembert's violin string, waves associated with atomic and nuclear phenomena and light waves. Light waves in particular are part and parcel of many natural phenomena. We are very fortunate to have one kind of phenomenon, waves, as the cornerstone of so many natural processes. Clearly the architect of the universe saw waves as a very useful concept as he went about his business; why did he choose waves for so many and such a variety of natural processes? Surely this choice should give us a penetrating glimpse into his nature. How do we find the key to this clue?

Of all the natural wave phenomena the very most important is almost certainly light. We owe our ability to understand and control light to James Clerk Maxwell. Maxwell was born in 1831 in Edinburgh, Scotland; he was educated at the University of Edinburgh, then at Cambridge. His elegant differential equations, which describe the space-time behavior of electromagnetic fields, appear on the first page of the introduction of this book. They first appeared in print in a series of papers which he delivered in the 1860's, and then in his definitive 'Treatise on Electricity and Magnetism'. Maxwell was a mathematical physicist of the same rank as Einstein and Newton. He died at Cambridge, at the young age of forty-eight, in 1879.

Maxwell's work with electromagnetic waves illuminated several dark corners of physics. **All** radiant energy that reaches our planet is encompassed by his equations. All man-made transmissions of information that employ light, radio, or television wavelengths are analyzed using his math. Even the alternating current power grid in this country and around the world obeys his equations. Without Maxwell's equations we would still be in the dark! It was Newton's calculus that enabled Maxwell to formulate his equations. Newton illuminated the dark corner of physics in which gravitational phenomena were to be found. Thanks to Newton we can explore space, predict the motion of heavenly bodies and analyze the dynamics of physical bodies moving on the surface of our planet. Newton's studies of light and optical telescopes paved the way for astronomers as well as for Maxwell.

These two men provided us with the tools to understand electricity, gravity and waves. Mankind's debt to these two giants is enormous. They made a beginning to understanding the properties of light, but there remained much about light that was yet to be discovered. We shall continue to travel the road of light in the next chapter.

Chapter Twelve

Astronomy and Cosmology

Light illuminates the mysteries of the Universe

Stop and think about the importance of light. We could not live without it's life-giving energy, warmth and illumination. Furthermore, in its broadest definition, light, that-is-to-say electromagnetic radiation, is the only energy we receive from outside our planetary environment. Buried within that energy is an enormous amount of information about our universe. With our telescopes and other sensors, including satellite sensors, we see, and now visit, the sun, the moon, and the other planets in our solar system. We see the stars in our own galaxy and their location; we see other galaxies and their location. We are able to analyze the starlight, and from the analysis we can determine the chemical constituents of our own star, the sun, and other stars. We are able to measure the distance to celestial objects and the velocity with which stars and galaxies are receding from us by the Doppler effect (red shift). From the spectra of the light from other stars we can determine their chemistry; from the motion of certain heavenly bodies and associated radiation we can infer the existence of black holes, all of this because our planet is bathed in radiation from the rest of our universe.

By running the scenario of receding heavenly bodies backward we can arrive at a moment of creation and the Big Bang. The "noise" of the Big Bang is still echoing, bouncing off the limits of the universe, and is detectable as residual noise in our microwave radio-frequency spectrum.

Is the fact that our world has this marvelous light-embodied set of clues a chance occurrence? Or were clues and keys placed here and there for us to find, to educate us in the ways of the Universe, clues in the light and keys to understanding those clues in the mathematics?

Some of Our Universe Is Missing!

At least, that is the opinion that has been held until recently by all (or nearly all) cosmologists. The theories of the fraction of a second following the instant the Big Bang was initiated call for a certain amount of material in the universe. The theory of the first few seconds, the subsequent expansion of the universe and the formation of the galaxies and their stars is very successful in matching its predictions with what our scientists observe in the heavens. This theory involves a very sophisticated picture of the childhood of the universe. When the infant universe was less than the size of a soccer ball (yes, that's right, about the size of a large orange) the theory says it experienced an "exponential" (we know what that means) expansion or "inflation" for a very brief period. The characteristics that would accompany that "inflation" match very well the structure of the observable galaxies and the variations in the microwave echo of the Big Bang. However, observations of the universe can account for only about one third of the matter in the universe that the theory calls for. There is a "matter gap". Where is the missing two thirds?

Scientists don't like holes in their theories so they fill the holes with mysterious fillers. They filled the "matter gap" with "dark matter": this filler is turning out to be as ephemeral as was the "ether". We digress for a moment to tell the story of the ether. When light was first recognized to be a wave phenomenon, and all other waves, such as sound waves, needed a material medium to transmit them; scientists invented an "ether" which was supposed to pervade the universe and enable the transmission of these light waves. Maxwell's equations showed that the velocity of light in vacuum was invariant, always the same, and, consequently, that there was no need for the "ether". However, Maxwell's theories were just that, theories, and the scientists of the day *knew* that light required a material medium for transmission. Wrong! A brilliant experiment by two men named Michelson and Morley established the absence of any ether and the fact that light traveled very nicely through empty space. (Science, back to the drawing board!)

Like the ether that was supposed to fill space in order to have electromagnetic radiation pass to us from the stars, scientists filled the matter gap in their theory with "dark matter". "Dark matter" because no one could see it or find it! But hold on a moment, the observed low density of the material in the universe, the matter gap, has an upside. The match between what our telescopes see and the inflation theory is best with just such a low density. But we can't have it both ways, can we? Or can we? Back to the drawing board again!

Lambda, the Cosmological Constant

Now the cosmologists discover that their theories of the origin, constitution and destination of the universe work very well if the missing dark matter is accounted for, i.e. replaced by, an enormous amount of energy which pervades all of space. The amount of energy is twice the amount that would be produced by converting all the stars, galaxies, interstellar dust and planets into pure energy. *The cosmologists call this mysterious

---

*Remember $E = mc^2$? This is Einstein's famous formula that equates energy and matter. It says that if we choose a certain amount of mass "m" and convert it to pure energy E; the amount of energy is equal to m times the square of the velocity of light (which is a very, very large number = 9 followed by 16 zeros meters squared/second squared). If twice all the mass of the universe were transformed into energy **that would be a whale of a lot of energy!**

pervasive energy "lambda" and, also, "the cosmological constant". This takes care of the undetectable dark matter. The lambda theory is being subscribed to by a rather large number of very respected cosmologists in spite of the fact that it has an echo of ether and dark matter about it. But let's suppose this theory stands the tests of time. Is the energy accessible? What is its nature? Is it in the form of a field? What is its purpose? *Why is it there? Why does energy replace the material that one would expect to be there?* Is this enormous amount of energy embodied somehow in the Creator himself? Or is it "just there"? Will we ever know? Are we meant to know?

Before we leave this fascinating subject we must mention one more clue that seems to have been dropped to help us learn and understand. The lambda conjecture, if we may call it that, arose as a result of the discovery of an anomaly in the rate of expansion of the universe. The rate of expansion had been believed to be slowing due to the mutual gravitational attraction of all the material in the universe. Wrong! (In fact, Very Wrong, we had it backwards!) Now we believe the expansion not to be slowing but to be accelerating! Is it being pushed by lambda?

How did we recognize the acceleration? We measure the distance to distant galaxies using the brightness, the "luminance", of exploding stars called supernovae. These celestial beacons have been described as "standard candles". Where does such a name come from? When the United States Bureau of Standards was faced many decades ago with the challenge of establishing a standard for illumination they defined a candle of certain dimensions, made of a certain wax, with a certain wick size, etc. The light emitted by that candle formed the standard for photometry. It was the "standard candle" and it had "one candlepower".

Well, it would take an infinity of U.S. standard candles to equal one supernova, but for the astronomer and cosmologist the supernova is a standard candle because, in every galaxy, they all have the same intrinsic brightness, the same "luminosity"! As the energy from these stars spreads out over the spherical surface of the space surrounding the star, over enormous distances; the stars appear to dim as the distance increases. So we can establish the distance to the supernova by its apparent brightness! No one has explained the remarkable consistency of the brightness of these beacons, but their reliability has been established over many years of many observations.

When observations of novae believed to be at a known distance were found to be dimmer than expected an effort was made to account for the extra dimness by clouds of intervening dust or other effects. None of these explanations stood up under scrutiny. The only explanation was that an enormous repulsive force was at work accelerating the expansion of the universe; the novae were farther away than previously believed! The lambda cosmological constant was the answer.

How did we get so lucky that these celestial standard candles were there to give us a clue to this fundamental property of the universe? No doubt astronomers would say that there is a perfectly rational explanation in terms of the form, amount and structure of the material that exploded into these supernovae; what else would you expect? Does that make it any less astounding? Was this astronomical convenience an accident of nature or was it established as an aid to Homo sapien's education? *What do you think?*

Before we say goodbye to the lambda cosmological constant we must recognize the possibility that there may be another explanation for the "dark matter". Several thousand feet below the surface of the earth, in an old Japanese zinc mine, there rests an experiment on the grand scale to measure the properties of the neutrino, a ubiquitous sub-atomic particle long believed to be whizzing through the earth, through each of us, unimpeded in its flight by virtue of having zero mass. The Super-Kamiokande experiment appears to have shattered that massless property of the neutrino and with it the so-called Standard Model of nuclear particles and forces. The neutrino mass, though very tiny (approximately 10,000,000 will weigh the same amount as an electron) appears to be finite. The universe is full of neutrinos, perhaps 100,000,000 per cubic meter of "empty space"! So, in the aggregate, there may be enough neutrinos to account for the dark matter. Whether neutrino or lambda or a combination of both or some third discovery chases the dark matter into oblivion, it appears to be on its way into the dustbin of physics along with the ether.

Chapter Thirteen

Force Fields

Gravity, magnetism, and electricity are all characterized by force fields. Force fields have some very, very mysterious properties! All of these fields exist in empty space (but is it really empty if the fields are there?). *Where there should be nothing, they are present!* This is *very* mysterious! There is energy stored in all force fields, and that energy can be drawn upon to perform useful work. The most intimate secrets of creation are tied to fields, to the gravitational field in particular.

Force fields are all around us. What are "force fields"? The best example of a force field is the field of gravity. It is the force that connects our feet to the floor and our tires to the road. It causes skiers to fly downhill. It takes energy to move these skiers downhill; the gravitational field supplies that energy. (The skiers must supply that energy from their bodies when they climb back uphill). Gravity, magnetism, and electricity all have associated fields; in some respects they are quite similar in their properties, in others very different. Gravity and electrostatics share a mathematically similar potential function. Electric fields can be stopped by a copper metallic shield, magnetic fields by an iron shield, but there seems to be no shield for gravity, we can not escape it, and that's a very good thing for us! **Should we suspect a benign exception?**

Energy is stored in force fields. We use the energy stored in the earth's magnetic field to move our compass needles. The gravitational field that exists between earth and moon was used in the Apollo Moon Program to provide some of the energy for the vehicles that carried Neil Armstrong and other astronauts from earth to moon and home again. Energy is stored in the field of an electromagnet, it makes our electric motors run. The electric fields that exist among earth and clouds in a thunder-storm store the energy we see in the electric discharges that are lightning. In our discussion of the "lambda constant" associated with the cosmology of the universe we learned that there may very well be an energy field pervading the universe that replaces the "dark matter". What a marvelous gift this will be if it exists and if we learn to draw energy from this source!

The most familiar force field is gravity. We all take gravity for granted, we seldom think about it, but we'd be in deep trouble without it! There are some very intriguing physical phenomena associated with gravity and, more important for us, some everyday properties without which we would not be here! We depend on gravity to keep us in contact with the ground, to keep our planet in orbit around the sun and to never change. But it does change, a very little bit, as we climb mountains, and our clocks respond to this! *Yes, our clocks run a little bit faster at the top of a mountain than they do at the bottom.* No need to reset your wristwatch; the change in clock rate can be detected only by highly precise "atomic clocks", but the change is there. In fact, the change can be detected between the top and the bottom of a one-hundred foot tower. Now this is very curious, to recognize that the flow of time is affected by gravity. Why? Is there some purpose for this phenomenon? What could it be? Clock-rates are also very much affected by observers moving with velocities approaching the velocities of light. Why is the flow of time variable under these conditions? Will we need to find a way to take advantage of it in order to escape our solar system and travel the universe? *Why is the flow of time the way it is?*

We know that light has no physical mass because, were a mass-particle to reach the velocity of light, its mass would becomes infinite; of course, this is not possible. The increase in mass of a high-speed particle was predicted by Einstein's Special Relativity and has been observed in our atom-smashers where particles are accelerated to speeds close to the velocity of light and their mass increases accordingly. Yet, massless light waves passing near the sun are deflected by the sun's enormous gravitational pull, by it's gravitational field. The images of stars whose positions are precisely known appear to have moved if their light passes close to the sun's limb during a solar eclipse; their light rays are bent by the sun. This fact was proof of Einstein's theories when observations were made during a solar eclipse early in the 20th century. A quantitative theory, General Relativity, explains the size of the effect in terms of a four-dimensional geometry, but leaves us with an uncomfortable feeling that we don't really understand what is going on! Einstein and his cosmological brethren seem to be able to account for some of its properties, but what *is* gravity? An esoteric theory may account for its behavior, *but what is it?*

We are all aware, also, of magnetism. Magnetism has some very curious properties. If we take a permanent bar magnet, having one north pole toward which a compass will point and one south pole, and then cut the bar magnet in half, *presto*, we find we have two magnets, two north poles and two south poles! Continuing this process delivers the same result. Very curious! Magnetic curiosities don't stop there. In the first quarter of the 19th century a man named Oersted discovered, more or less accidentally, that when he caused a steady current to flow in a wire by connecting the wire to the terminals of a battery, the needle of a nearby compass would deflect in a direction at right angles to the wire while the current was flowing!

This was a very unexpected occurrence and it is extremely curious! It is this fortunate phenomenon which permits engineers to design electric motors. Electric motors provide a source of power that can be localized at each machine in our factories; a source of power which need be no larger than the machine requires and which can be turned off when not in use. Before electric motors were available a large power source (water wheel or steam engine) distributed power to machines by way of shafts and pulleys. This method of distributing power was both very inefficient and very awkward, but steam and water power were the first wave of the industrial revolution. The electric motor was the second; it revolutionized manufacturing. What a gift! The next time you look at an electric motor, show a little respect. Tip your hat, and be grateful!

An electron at rest is unaffected by a magnetic field, but, once the electron starts to move, the magnetic field causes the electron to move at a right angle to both its instantaneous direction of motion and the direction of the magnetic field. This fortunate phenomenon permits us all to enjoy television (a stream of electrons aimed at the screen is moved about by magnetic fields and paints the TV picture). Electrons and other charged particles moving in combined electric and magnetic fields can be made to whirl round and round an invisible racetrack and smash atoms; scientists examine the debris and construct theories of atomic and nuclear structure. This phenomenon of the behavior of charged particles has become old-hat, but stop and think about it for a moment, it is weird behavior, not what one would expect. Why is nature being so helpful? Does someone want to educate us? Does someone *want* us to understand the atom and its nucleus? Is the Creator in charge of our curriculum?

We have all experienced the effects of the electric fields associated with alternating current. These cause our automobile radios to encounter static as we drive near a power transmission line. Some of us have experienced the static electricity fields (not to be confused with the radio static, of course) that cause our hair to stand on end when we encounter the right atmospheric conditions at the Grand Canyon. So these fields are familiar to us. But, what are they? We know their effects, but we don't know what they are! Our scientists can compute their strength and successfully predict their effects, thank goodness, because many of the conveniences in our lives depend on this ability, but that is not to say that we know what they are!

Light is a form of energy that propagates by virtue of an electro-magnetic field, a field which contains both electric and magnetic energy. A ray of light from a distant star isn't really a ray, it is an electromagnetic wave. The portion of the light which reaches our eye is part of an enormous plane surface of electromagnetic wave energy moving toward us from the star (the "ray" is really just a line joining the center of our eye to the center of the star and that line is perpendicular to the plane surface or "wave front"). The surface of the wave is not really plane, the surface is a huge spherical surface, but the star is so distant that the portion of the wavefront which reaches the earth is indistinguishable from a plane wavefront. The pupil of our eye intercepts the electromagnetic energy of a small area of this plane surface and forms an image of the star on our retina. That is the reason we can all see the same star at the same time; each eye intercepts a small area of the huge plane surface over which the light energy is uniformly distributed.

We see that there are two types of fields, "static", in other words unchanging, and "dynamic" or changing, fluctuating. A simple example will make the difference clear. As we have seen, Oersted discovered that when he caused a steady current to flow in a wire by connecting the wire to the terminals of a battery, the needle of a nearby compass would deflect while the current was flowing. As long as the wire and compass were motionless and the current was steady the compass needle was motionless; the situation was unchanging, i.e. "static". Another scientist of the 19th century named Heinrich Hertz discovered, about the time of our Civil War, that when a current flowing in a wire was rapidly reversed in direction another wire located somewhat remotely from the first would conduct a current sympathetically, with reversals occurring at the same frequency as the reversals in the first. There was a "dynamic" action at a distance caused by the fluctuating current! Thanks to this gift we are able to communicate today over long distances by radio, wireless, and television. Thanks to the combined efforts of physicists and mathematicians we are able to analyze, predict the behavior and make beneficial use of gravity, magnetism, electricity, and electromagnetic waves. But they are never-the-less mysterious, and their behavior greatly surprised those who first encountered them.

Are these marvelous gifts of gravity, magnetism, electricity and electro-magnetic waves evidence that somebody up there likes us? Or is it just chance? What do you think?

Chapter Fourteen

The Tiny World

All around us there is a Lilliputian world we can not see. That rocky prominence in a cliff face is really mostly empty space. It is a collection of protons and whirling electrons; a flood of neutrinos are whizzing through it; It consists of different chemical entities which, in turn, consist of atoms. We call the basic building blocks of nature "atoms"; there are a few more than 100 of these materials with a few less than 100 occurring naturally in nature. From these few different components nature and man have assembled a myriad of substances. The rock is composed of atoms; so is the very air we breathe. The air is a gas composed mostly of atoms of oxygen and nitrogen. The simplest of all atoms is the hydrogen atom; its diameter is approximately one ten thousandth of one millionth of a meter (a meter is about a yard long). It *is* tiny. How many atoms of hydrogen do you consume with every drop of water? Billions! Other atoms are larger; gold atoms are about 300 times as large as a hydrogen atom, but they are still very tiny. It is only in the last few centuries that we have had the mathematics to unlock the mysteries concealing this tiny universe. Let's take a look at this fascinating world. Here the Creator was building the foundations for the universe. Here, if anywhere, there are sure to be some clues.

Atoms and Molecules

Chemistry is the science of the marriage, divorce and remarriage of atoms; the marital state is known as a molecule. When atmospheric oxygen mates with iron we get rust molecules, and when hydrogen atoms form a lasting relationship with oxygen atoms we get water molecules. As everyone knows, a water molecule, H2O, consists of two atoms of hydrogen and one of oxygen. Every molecule of a substance is composed of atoms; so atoms are the basic building blocks that form the substances that are the subject of chemistry. The distinctions between chemistry and physics have blurred as scientists have discovered the behavioral secrets of atoms and molecules, but the number of substances and the related body of knowledge that is the realm of chemistry is so vast that it is still proper to identify it as a separate science. There are a few more than a hundred different kinds of atoms and most of them are willing, more often than not demanding, to form bonds with other atoms, including multiple bonds. Atoms are a promiscuous lot and the number of combinatorial permutations and combinations that are possible is almost without limit.

The history of chemistry discloses some fascinating and curious discoveries, and we shall spend a moment reviewing a few of the most interesting of these on the road to the present. A good place to start is Avogadro's hypothesis. Very early in the 19th century an Italian physicist named Avogadro proposed a theory that equal volumes of **different** gases contained the same number of molecules when the equal volumes were at the same temperature and pressure, say, zero degrees Centigrade and one atmosphere. How in the world would anyone come to that conclusion? Well, he performed experiments of the following nature. Take two volumes of hydrogen and one volume of oxygen, mix them and presto!: two volumes of steam! Not three, but two, and no leftovers! The conclusion must be that the number of water molecules in the steam is the same as the number of hydrogen molecules (each molecule of hydrogen contains two atoms and likewise each molecule of oxygen contains two atoms). Two molecules of hydrogen combine with one molecule of oxygen to make two molecules of steam. Each molecule of steam contains two atoms of hydrogen and one atom of oxygen. That's a lot of atomic and molecular bookkeeping!

The apparatus for performing experiments like Avogadro's is known as a Eudiometer; it consists of a tube partially filled with mercury into which the gases are introduced. The chemical reaction is set off by a spark from an induction coil. The chemistry book says, "If exact proportions of the gases are used the mercury completely fills the tube after the reaction, but is apt to break it by striking the top violently!. In other words a lovely explosion!" No wonder it is easy to interest young boys (and girls) in chemistry!

The next obvious question is "How many molecules are there in a given size container at standard conditions of temperature and pressure?" Answer: if the container is a cube about eleven inches on a side, there are about 6 followed by 23 zeros molecules inside! That's a lot. 6.022 times 10 to the 23'd power (6.022×10^{23}) in the mathematical notation we now know is the exact value for Avogadro's number. Although this fundamental number is named after Avogadro, he did not discover it. The exact number is named after him in honor of the discovery that there are the same number of molecules of any gas in a given volume container under the same conditions of temperature and pressure! Why? One would just not expect that a light gas like helium and a heavy gas like mercury vapor would share this common characteristic. Very curious.

This kind of combinatorial experimentation and analysis was then applied by John Dalton. He discovered that chemical reactions tend to take place when the constituents are simple integer multiples of each other, 1:1, 2:1, 3:2 etc. He was then able to establish the number of atoms in various molecules and from this to set up a table of relative atomic weights. Now, the curious phenomenon to be emphasized here is the simplicity of these relationships. It is as if someone *wanted* us to find them and to learn to use these keys to molecules and atoms to master chemistry and all the good products and materials that flow to us Homo sapiens as a consequence of this knowledge.

Or is it just a result of we humans being very smart and nature being nature? What do you think?

Einstein and the Photoelectric Effect

Albert Einstein was born in 1879 to Hermann and Pauline Einstein in the German city of Ulm. Five years later he was joined by a sister Maria, always called 'Maja', to whom he was very close all of his life. His skull at birth was very unusually shaped and remained so. He did not speak until well after a normal period for children. He preferred to play by himself, did well in school, learned to play the violin, and was given to occasional tantrums. In 1896 he abandoned his German citizenship. In 1901 he became a Swiss citizen. He was educated at ETH, the "Hochschule" in Zurich. Employed at the patent office in 1902, he was able to marry Mileva Maric in 1903; they had two sons.

In 1905 he published several papers which astounded the world of physics: A paper on the light quantum (photo-electric effect); two papers on Brownian Motion; two papers on special relativity, the second of which contained the famous equation $E = mc^2$. About a year after these remarkable achievements, Einstein, who worked in the Swiss patent office, was promoted to technical expert *second class* and given a raise in pay. The promotion was unrelated to his ground-breaking papers in physics; he was recognized for his performance as a patent technologist. He was pleased with the promotion and the pay increase.

In 1922 Einstein was awarded the Nobel Prize for his explanation of the photo-electric effect, he had indeed graduated to first class!

In spite of his crucial contributions to quantum physics, Einstein was never comfortable with the role of chance in the micro-world (about which more later); he never abandoned his commitment to causality. He did not see "God playing at dice". After a second marriage and a final position at Princeton University, he died April 18, 1955. His body was cremated and the ashes scattered. He was a giant among us, an intellect which appears only once in hundreds of years.

The photoelectric effect, its discovery, and the consequences of that discovery are one of the most fascinating and curious tales in physics. We have mentioned the experiments of Heinrich Hertz that resulted in the discovery of radio waves. In the course of his experimentation he observed that the voltage (the electrical force) necessary to cause a spark to jump from one metal electrode to another was diminished when ultraviolet light was illuminating the electrodes! Now, that is pretty curious! Then a decade later, in 1898, a physicist named J. J. Thomson discovered that a metal plate illuminated with ultraviolet light emitted negative electric charges. That is even more curious! (J. J. Thomson was director of the Cavendish laboratory at Cambridge University in England and is credited with the discovery of the electron). The emission of these negative charges did not occur when the plate was illuminated with "white" light, no matter how intense the illumination! Further experimentation showed that different metals exhibited different "photoelectric thresholds". Some materials were willing to shed electrons only under the illumination from the very short waves in the invisible ultraviolet; other more cooperative materials would give up their electrons at the longer waves in the blue end of the visible spectrum. This curious effect was explained by Einstein in 1905; he proposed that the light energy falling on the plate consisted of short trains of sinusoidal (see Fig. 20) waves called quanta and that the short wavelength packets (or trains) contained more energy than the long wavelength packets. (The short wavelength packets contain more wave crests per unit of time than the long wavelength packets; just like sound waves of high pitch contain more vibrations per second, more wave crests, than sound waves of low pitch).

The short wavelength packets contained sufficient energy to dislodge the electrons from the plate. Each electron was released from the plate by a single quantum of light! It is a characteristic of the photo-electric effect that the shorter the wavelength of the light the more vigorous the electron emission; the electron leaves the metal plate with increasing speed as the wavelength of the light decreases. But no electrons will leave the metal until they receive enough energy to lift them above a barrier characteristic of each metal; until the wavelength of the light is short enough to lift them over the threshold. Clearly, the energy in each quantum increases as the quantum's wavelength decreases!

We have all seen the electric charge on a comb or on our clothing attract a bit of paper, and it is often a struggle to make "popcorn" packing material let go of our hands because of the electric charge on the surface of the "kernel of popcorn". In these instances we think of electrons as tiny particles at rest. However, electrons in motion behave very much like light waves; they exhibit behavior that can be accounted for only by waves. So which are they, are they tiny point particles or are they waves? Answer: they are both!

How can this be? In 1924 a French graduate student was writing his doctorate thesis at the University of Paris. He was a French aristocrat named Prince Louis de Broglie. His elder brother was a well-known physicist who had done some important work in x-rays. At the age of nineteen Louis listened to his brother deliver a speech on some of the mysterious properties of light; he became interested in the subject and decided to study physics. He was very much intrigued with the dual nature of light. At this time there was ample evidence that it behaved as waves at some times and as particles at other times. He was preoccupied with this strange characteristic of nature; then, in a flash of brilliance, de Broglie extended the duality concept to matter! In particular he proposed that there was a wavelength associated with an electron in motion, and that the wavelength was inversely proportional to its momentum; i.e. inversely proportional to its velocity since the electron mass is constant; the slower the electron the longer its associated wavelength. Under this concept the wavelength of an electron at rest is infinite: point charge at rest, very, very long wavelength. Then as the electron picks up speed the wavelength becomes shorter and shorter until at high speeds the wavelength is so short that the electron exhibits many of the characteristics of a photon of light. Louis predicted that electrons in motion would exhibit the same diffraction properties that light exhibits, and of course he was correct.

The electron has some further surprises for us! It exhibits the characteristics of a tiny charged body rotating about an axis; it behaves like a tiny top (has angular momentum) and also behaves like a tiny magnet. It is said by physicists to have "spin". It turns out that other tiny components of atoms exhibit "spin" also. One of the curious features of the atom is a component of the atomic nucleus called the neutron; "neutron" because it has no charge. **But** the neutron does have spin and behaves like a magnet in spite of the fact that it shows no charge! Unlike the top we all played with as children, the spin of the electron and the neutron never decrease. Where does the energy come from to keep it going? Or does it spin without losing energy! Is this an exception to our ordinary experience with nature? Or does our concept of "spin" have a flaw in it? No one is sure. How can all this be? There is no answer to that question except to say, "That's the way the Creator did it!".

As we have noted, light, like the electron, behaves in two ways: sometimes its behavior is accounted for by rays, the passage of particles, and sometimes by waves. Again, it is not one or the other; it is both. Nature does not require that we be comfortable with a contradiction like that. This is an *uncomfortable discovery*, and we may as well get used to it; there is nothing we can do about it, except wonder, and ask *Why?* We Homo sapiens have an unfortunate history of exhibiting serious problems when dealing with really new ideas, uncomfortable ideas. The Pythagoreans could not accept irrational numbers. The idea that the sun, not the earth, was the center of the universe (as it was then conceived) was to lead many to the terrors of the Inquisition. It flew in the face of the dogma of the Catholic Church; it flew in the face of what the Church *knew* that God had done, what He had created. The idea that there must be a material medium for the transmission of electromagnetic waves led to the creation of the non-existent "ether" because the physicists of that day *knew* that the natural world required it. The idea that there *must* be more matter in the universe than could be observed led to the creation of what is apparently non-existent dark matter. What is it about us Homo sapiens that makes us so reluctant to accept that which nature tries to tell us? Even the brilliant

Einstein was reluctant to accept a fundamental element in the quantum theory; that chance was at the heart of nature. **But,** to the best of our current knowledge, he made a correct guess that the universe was filled with energy, then cast it aside since it conflicted with the observations of the astronomers of that time. That Einstein was smart!

Light at the Atomic Scale, Atomic Spectra

Light illuminates not only our knowledge of the dark recesses of the universe but also our knowledge of the nature of the atom. Near the turn of the century, about 100 years ago, scientists observed that when the light from an incandescent gas was passed through a narrow slit and then through a glass prism the light was separated into a series of bright lines of different colors. The lines were separated by dark intervals, each bright line being an image of the slit. The name "line spectrum" has been given to this display of light spread out into "color bars". See Fig. 21.

LINE SPECTRUM, BALMER SERIES, HYDROGEN

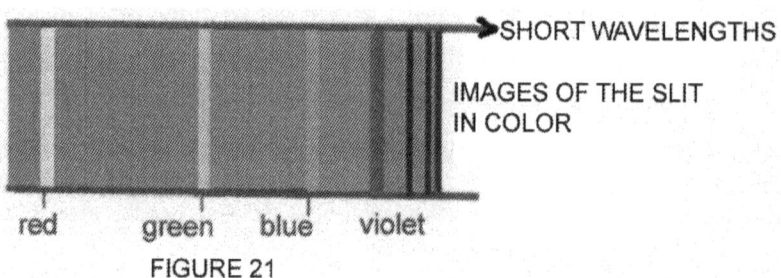

red   green blue violet

FIGURE 21

No one could account for this strange phenomenon until a young Danish scientist named Niels Bohr proposed a theory that each atom is composed of a central nucleus around which whirl a number of electrons, each electron in a stationary orbit. The number of electrons per atom depends upon the material in the incandescent gas.This model can be compared to our solar system where the sun is the "nucleus" and the planets are the "electrons".

Niels Bohr was born in Copenhagen on October 7, 1885. The Bohrs were a prosperous middle class Danish family; head of the family was Christian Bohr, a well-regarded physiologist. Niels mother was Jewish; she and Christian had another son, Harald, who made a name for himself in mathematics. The Bohr family traveled in an intellectual segment of Danish society. Both Niels and his brother were accomplished athletes and especially good at soccer. Niels was educated at the University of Copenhagen. In 1911 Bohr found his way to the Cavendish Laboratory in Cambridge where he worked for a time under J. J. Thomson, discoverer of the electron. In 1912 he married Margarethe Norlund; she was very bright and Bohr often sought her advice.

Bohr was led to a successful model of the atom by a formula for the spacing of the spectral lines of hydrogen; this famous formula was discovered by a Swiss high-school teacher named Johann Balmer. The spacing of the lines is governed by the orbital transitions of the electron in the hydrogen atom. As a consequence of his atomic model, Bohr became a leader in the world of twentieth century physics; his intellect and character were much admired by his peers. After a storybook escape from Denmark to Sweden as he was pursued by the Nazis, he joined the atomic bomb effort at Los Alamos. He returned to Denmark in 1945. He was awarded a Nobel Prize in 1922. He died in 1962, age 78.

There is a charming and well-known story about Bohr and his sense of humor. He had as a guest in his home a prominent member of the scientific community. This guest noticed that on the door of Bohr's summer-house he had placed a horseshoe. He asked Bohr if he believed that horseshoes affixed to doors brought good luck. Bohr replied, "Of course not, but I've been told that they bring good luck even to those who do not believe".

In the Bohr model the electrons in the atom are restricted to orbits at fixed distances from the nucleus. Associated with each orbit is a different energy level. The electrons may move from one orbit to another when they receive or give up a quantum of energy. A quantum of energy is a tiny amount of electromagnetic energy. This amount of energy is known to physicists as "hf" where h is Planck's constant (h = 6.6262×10^{-27} erg-seconds) and f is the frequency of the light, (for visible light f = 5×10^{14} waves per second). The energy in one quantum of green light is about 3×10^{-12} ergs of energy, or about three millionths of a millionth of an erg. One erg is one ten-millionth of one watt-second, you are familiar with watt-hours if you pay your light bills. The energy in a quantum of green light is very small indeed, and you get a lot of them for your monthly electric bill! The amount of energy in the quantum depends upon the wavelength. Much, but not all, of light energy is in the visible portion of the electromagnetic spectrum. The shorter the wavelength the more energy in a quantum, blue light has more energy than green, green has more energy than red.

There are two types of atomic spectra: emission spectra and absorption spectra. The emission spectra have been described in the preceding paragraphs. However, atoms may absorb as well as emit energy. If light coming from a source that contains all wavelengths passes through a gas, then through a slit and a glass prism, a series of dark "absorption lines" appear in a color spectrum that extends from dark red to violet. Certain of the wavelengths of the incident light have "excited" the atoms in the gas and their energy has been removed from the totality of wavelengths that were incident on the gas. The absorption lines for a given gas, say hydrogen, will have the same location in the spectrum as the hydrogen emission lines. Light from the sun that passes through a slit and prism exhibits such dark absorption lines.

That characteristic of light that provides for very pure single wavelength energy has bestowed upon us a remarkable capability: lasers. Lasers take advantage of the properties of atomic energy transitions to provide us with precision metal cutting devices, delicate surgical instruments to correct our vision, surveying instruments, laser-guided missiles, optical instruments that make possible the precise and accurate figuring of optical surfaces (such as those in the orbiting Hubble telescope) and many more marvelous tools.

The basic idea incorporated in a laser takes advantage of the fact that reflected light waves will travel back and forth between two highly reflecting mirrors which are opposite each other and which are spaced by some multiple of the desired light wavelength. In this sense the light wave 'resonates' like the resonance of a pure tone sound wave in an organ pipe. (We see another manifestation of the commonality in nature). The laser encloses the mirrors in an evacuated cavity that is partially filled with a gas the atoms of which can be stimulated to a high energy level by an energy "pump" light. The excited atoms then fall to a lower energy level emitting a pure wavelength of light in sync with the light wave that is bouncing back and forth between the two mirrors. Because of this synchronous condition the light emitted by each atom reinforces the laser beam. One of the mirrors has a partially reflecting surface that permits what we see as the laser beam to escape.

We see the discrete side of nature at work in atomic spectra. Through the dominant role that the mathematics of probability plays in atomic physics we use the power of discrete mathematics to understand and predict behavior at the atomic level.

The Bohr model of the atom and its behavior was an enormous step forward in our understanding of atomic physics. However, it is only an approximation to what scientists now believe to be the actual state of affairs. The atomic structure and its behavior is much more complex than is predicted by the Bohr model. It remained for the discovery of quantum mechanics to improve the model.

What is quantum mechanics? It is the mathematics that enables us to understand the tiny world of atomic and nuclear physics; a world in which particles and energy come in quanta or discrete packets (some might say 'lumps') as distinct from the way things in the macro world appear to be composed of continuous matter. A man named Paul A. M. Dirac discovered that a non-commutative algebra was key to understanding quantization. What in the world is non-commutative algebra? It is an algebra in which the order in which things are taken makes a difference! A times B is not the same as B times A! Dirac was the son of a Swiss father and an English mother. He was born in Bristol England in 1902. He was educated in mathematics at St. John's College, Cambridge. He played a key role in the development of quantum mechanics. We pause to take note of non-commutative algebra in order to emphasize that in the tiny world of atoms and their components things are different! We shall leave it at that for the moment. Dirac made great contributions to physics and mathematics and occupied the Lucasian Chair of Mathematics at Cambridge University, the chair Newton occupied nearly three hundred years before him.

Can we be sure that the quantum mechanical model is not simply an improved approximation? We can not!

Quantum Physics

Each atom can exist in a very large number of different energy states. These states are defined by the states of the electrons. Each electron can exist in a multitude of different states, so an atom has a very large choice of different configurations. Not all of these configurations have different energy levels, but very many do. When the energy level in an atom changes, light, or electromagnetic energy, is emitted or absorbed and the wavelength, or color, of the light is determined very precisely by the change of energy level. Scientists are able to measure those wavelengths very accurately. With a great deal of effort atomic physicists have been able to establish mathematical models of the atoms which predict the wavelengths for all, or almost all, of the many transitions. Homo sapiens' ability to make successful predictions of atomic behavior depends on Quantum Mechanics; and Quantum Mechanics depends on an equation discovered by a German physicist named Erwin Schrodinger.

The principle variable in Schroedinger's equation is designated by the Greek letter "psi". Although Schroedinger's equation is much more complex, psi plays a similar mathematical role to the "y" of the wave equation we studied in Chapter 11. The initial triumph of Schroedinger's equation was that it gave results in numbers that agreed for the first time with experimental data. However, no one, including Schroedinger, knew what psi represented! The finest minds in physics were stumped! Did it relate to the density of electric charge in the atom? What was psi? The puzzle was ultimately resolved by discovering that the psi quantity related to the *probability* that the electron would be found in a certain tiny volume of space. This story describes a situation frequently encountered in math and science; often the solution to a problem precedes a complete understanding of the solution.

Although Schrodinger's equation has the same form as the wave equations which describe many natural phenomena, it does not describe a physical wave phenomenon. Instead, it makes possible the calculation of the *probability* of the existence of different atomic states. It is the transitions from one of these states to another that creates the emission of light that we see in atomic spectra. Schrodinger's equation permits us to correctly predict the wavelength of these spectra. Again we see the commonality of various physical properties in terms of the mathematics which relate to them! The Creator must have liked the way that the wave equation applied to the macroscopic world so he applied it to the microscopic world in the form of the determination of atomic state probabilities. And he was wild about quanta! The farther we probe into the tiny world of atoms, nuclei, protons, pions, quarks, antimatter and the remaining host of particles and their parents and offspring, the more and more quanta we encounter. Mathematics continues to be the dominant tool with which we attempt to understand this tiny world.

Light plays a role in revealing to us the structure of the building blocks of the universe. However, there are still plenty of mysteries! Why is it the electrons can continue in their circular atomic orbits with no loss of energy? Electromagnetic theory requires that an accelerating electron must radiate electromagnetic energy (light). Circular motion is accompanied by acceleration, which you can verify by whirling a stone at the end of a string and experiencing the force on your arm needed to counteract the accelerating mass of the stone. In a cyclotron, where the electrons whirl in a large circular orbit, they lose energy by radiation. Why not in the atom? How does nature manage to have it both ways?

The world of the miniscule: the atom, the electron, the neutron and the proton, and the neighboring world of quanta: of photons, of electron spin, of cosmic rays and of bosons and fermions is a world where chance rules.

Chapter Fifteen

Chance—It Makes Us Lucky

Those who see the hand of God in every aspect of human life must see his hand rolling the dice! The most fundamental thrusts in nature: quantum mechanics, mutation, evolution, are all driven by chance occurrences. But these chance occurrences, at least in physics and in gambling, result in highly predictable effects! How can this be? How can micro-chance lead to macro-certainty? The answer is that in the aggregate not all these chance occurrences are equally likely, equally probable. **Did somebody load the cosmic dice?**

Gambling casinos don't have to load the dice, they simply choose the probabilities they wish and then design the game accordingly, e.g. "set the odds in the slot machine". Las Vegas prospers because the outcome of many, many rolls of the dice, or turns of the cards in blackjack, is very certain. The laws of chance have no memory. Roll five sevens and the odds for the next roll to be a seven are no different than they were on the first roll. Some gambler may have a hot hand for a short time, and he may think the dice have a memory, but over the long term the probabilities associated with "games of chance" govern the outcome. For the player, games of chance are not games of chance at all; he is a certain loser and the house a certain winner. Seven is more probable than a five when the (honest) dice are rolled, and in a full well-shuffled deck a face card is more probable than a six. Always.

Let's see how this works, because in the realm of the tiny, the realm of quantum mechanics, this *is* the way it works. (A reminder here, remember

Avogadro's number, that a shoe box of gas atoms contains a number of atoms equal to about 10 followed by 23 zeros, When we deal with atoms, electrons, protons etc. we have to work with ***huge*** numbers. A billion billion of something gets lost because there is so little of it!)

Consider a Head/Tails game in which N pennies are tossed simultaneously and then the number of heads is counted (The number of tails will be N minus the number of heads of course). Let's say N=10; there are 10 coins, how likely is it that all coins will be heads? All tails? Not very. How likely that there will be 5 heads and 5 tails? Much more likely. Four heads and 6 tails is almost but not quite as likely, and three heads and seven tails even less likely.As the number of coins becomes very large: 1000, 10,000, a million, the results will cluster around an even head/tails split. As the number of games (in which all coins are tossed simultaneously) increases, the distribution of total results will cluster very sharply around half heads and half tails.

Let's ask how long it would take if one million trillion coins were tossed simultaneously, once every second, before all coins would come up heads on two successive tosses? The answer is undoubtedly a length of time that exceeds by far the age of the universe; it will never happen. This is the meaning of "Never". The converse, that it will never happen, is certain. On the other hand, if there are only five coins in the toss, all heads on two successive tries may take some time but it will surely happen, probably in less than a day. So, when we deal with the behavior of a few atoms or molecules their behavior has a certain degree of uncertainty about it, but when there are a shoe box full, about 10 followed by twenty three zeros according to Avogadro's number; their aggregate behavior is certain.

Now, as we stop to think about this for a moment, we can convince ourselves with little difficulty that a world in which chance rules in the way it does is a very certain, a very safe world! What a wonderful way to make most things we deal with in our daily lives very predictable,**and still include the possibility of occasional change!** Why is this the way things are? How did this very curious and wonderful set of circumstances happen?

But in this chancy world there are some things that are certain. As an example we'll take a look at the Pauli Exclusion Principle. If that doesn't intimidate the reader nothing will! But as you will see there is little to fear. (W. Pauli made many contributions to atomic physics in the nineteen twenties; his discovery of the exclusion principle is of enormous importance). Every electron in an atom, as it does its dance around the atomic nucleus, is characterized by a set of several numbers called quantum numbers. They are designated by letters (say, k,l,m,n,). Each letter can take on multiple values as the electron finds itself in different "quantum states".[*] The set of quantum numbers depends on the position of the electron with respect to the nucleus and many other things as well, but for our purposes it is sufficient to say that a set of perhaps four numbers characterize the electron's condition at a given instant of time. As the atom receives or gives up energy, for example, these numbers may change, but the *number* of quantum numbers will not.

Pauli's principle says that no two electrons in one atom can have the same set of quantum numbers, **not ever**, in all the zillions of atoms of that element in the universe! (No double occupancy in the hotel!). So, not everything is chancy, there are safeguards built into the system which assure a basic stability which underlies the role of chance. In a similar way the velocity of light in empty space has a constant value that can never be exceeded. There are some certainties in our probabilistic universe. Is that a neat system or what?

Before we leave the tiny world of atomic physics we need to think about what has brought us to this point where we have a very firm grasp of

---

[*]It is as if the electron was in a very large unoccupied hotel; it has it's choice of any room in the building, i.e. any quantum state, and will change rooms as the energy from a light quantum is emitted or absorbed. There is an exception as we shall see in the next paragraph.

the workings of this world. It appears that nature has been constructed in such a way that her atomic mysteries could be unraveled by us, by Homo sapiens, with a lot of effort, but within our capabilities. Who is vain enough to say that *any* world conceived of by the Creator, no matter how complex, could have been analyzed with a 1500 cubic centimeter brain?

Does this synergy between our capabilities and the comprehensibility of our world not seem predetermined? This is the Eternal Mystery!

Were we not fortunate to have Avogadro's hypothesis and the subsequent molecular/atomic discoveries of Dalton form a simple foundation for the revelations that followed? Atomic physics has been typified by a sequence of discoveries that began with the simple and proceeded to the more and more complex. There are over a hundred distinct atomic elements which vary from very light elements such as hydrogen and helium to very heavy elements such as gold and uranium. Initial discoveries were clustered in the simpler and plentiful elements: hydrogen, helium, oxygen, carbon and so on. The hydrogen atom is similar to our earth-moon system. It has a nucleus (earth) and one electron (moon); but there the analogy with our planet and its satellite stops. The moon orbits the earth in a plane, but when it is in its "normal" or "ground" state the electron orbits the hydrogen nucleus within a spherical volume that extends far from the nucleus. The electron can be found anywhere within that volume and over time it will trace out a path that forms sort of a mushy poorly defined ball, very much like a ball of string which is more dense toward the center than toward the outside of the ball. But the position of the electron within this volume is known only in terms of a likelihood, a probability. In this sense, its position depends on chance. The next element in terms of complexity is helium which has a nucleus and two electrons. These simplest structures were the focus of the initial experimentation and theoretical studies that provided the foundation for understanding the properties of the totality of elements.

What was the compass that enabled the early explorers to navigate this strange and inaccessible world? That compass was atomic spectra, the light emitted by excited atoms in highly selective well defined different colors (wavelengths) that revealed the structural secrets of these tiny worlds. ***Light and mathematics*** have been the keys to our understanding of much of the physical world. Is this not a great gift? Well, maybe not, maybe it is just a consequence of our large brains that we owe to switching from a vegetarian to a high-protein diet. What do you think?

Chapter Sixteen

Biotechnology

We Homo sapiens, with our opposed thumb, large brains, sexual reproduction and ability to form large cooperative groups, may be nature's greatest mystery. How did we get to be the way we are? How did we evolve? What is the composition of this organism that dominates the planet; how does it function? Does it have the god-like powers to influence the direction in which it will develop in the future?

We are an assembly of atoms all of which once formed part of a star. Some assemblies have retained this star quality and are more visually appealing than others, which accrues to the advantage of Hollywood and Victoria's Secret, but we are all made from the same materials. We consist of water molecules and a large number of *very* complex, very large molecules which carry exotic labels such as proteins, DNA, RNA, genes, etc. These molecules are organic in nature, that is to say they are based on carbon, oxygen, nitrogen and hydrogen with a liberal sprinkling of many other elements. Our knowledge of this world within our bodies is very recent, many of the watershed discoveries having been made in the last half of the twentieth century.

Many other objects, inanimate objects, are an assembly of atoms, objects like stones or steel, and yet they are not living, where we mean by living the ability to reproduce. By reproduction we mean the ability of an organism to create progeny which are similar to (not necessarily identical to) the parent. Being able to reproduce is a necessary but not sufficient criterion to characterize a living organism in the sense that we use the term here. Certain viruses are able to reproduce given the right environment, but they do not ingest substances (food), derive energy from the food, and secrete other substances. The viruses seem to be identical with each other and when they reproduce the reproductions are exact copies (in the absence of mutation). Living organisms, like plants or animals, ingest food, metabolize the food, repair damage, and produce offspring. Where does the spark of life originate that endows the living organism with "life"? Why doesn't the virus posses this spark? Why is the life characteristic of an animal different from the life characteristic of a vegetable; where does the difference originate and why?

The cell is fundamental to a living plant or animal. The plant or animal consists of a collection of cells of many different kinds, but the form and structure of these cells is similar. Be reminded that in a human being the cells consist of an outer wall within which a fluid called the cytoplasm surrounds the central cell nucleus. The chromosomes and genes that make us what we are reside in the cell, in every cell in our bodies, from the moment of conception. There are many different kinds of cells in the human body, but every human starts as a single cell! As the growth from this single cell progresses the multiplicity of different cells needed to create a fully functional Homo sapien are produced; presumably under the control of the genes. What is a gene? A gene is a large molecule, it is the key to inheritance. Genes are located on a chromosome. A chromosome is a very long chain of genes that are strung along it like the beads on a necklace. We Homo sapiens have 23 pairs of more or less rod-shaped chromosomes of which 22 come in pairs which are very similar, the 23'd depends on the sex of the individual who bears it. In women the 23'd pair is labeled xx by scientists; with respect to sex determination the two members of the pair are the same. In men the 23'd pair is labeled xy, the two members of the pair are different. If the y member of the pair dances with the female x the result is a male; if the x member does the tango with the female x the result is a female.

Each of us inherits half of each of our 23 chromosomes from our mother and half from our father; in this way we receive genes from each which determine our characteristics. I believe it was George Bernard Shaw who is said to have had a conversation on this subject with his beautiful significant other. She said, "Let's have a child; with my looks and your brains it would be exceptional." Shaw's reply, "But suppose, my dear, that the child had my looks and your brains!"

Each gene is a region, a portion, of a larger molecule of DNA. How many genes do we have? An enormous number, nearly 100,000! Each gene is a coded message and usually encodes the instructions for making one protein. Proteins carry out the functions that make our bodies work. For example, hemoglobin, a constituent of our red blood cells, is an iron containing protein which combines reversibly with oxygen; it collects oxygen from the lungs and carries it to the tissues in our bodies where food is oxidized ("burned"). Then the red cell is recirculated to the lung for another load of oxygen.

Genes are composed of DNA which is an acronym for deoxyribonucleic-acid. (What a mouthful, we'll stick with the acronym).

The DNA in each gene carries the information our bodies need to function. DNA is composed of four organic acids called nucleotides. For those of you who may remember a bit of chemistry the nucleotides are composed of a sugar, a phosphate group and a nitrogenous base. It is this base on which we shall focus since it carries the information in the DNA molecule. There are four different bases and four letters that are used to identify them: A, G, C, and T. These bases occur in a sequence of pairs. Each pair can be compared to a letter of the alphabet; the sequences of pairs spell out "words", just like a sequence of alphabetical letters. The "words" form coded commands that generate the thousands of different proteins our bodies need to function. The total number of base pairs in a human probably exceeds several billion. Unless you are an identical twin you are certain to be unique!

Base A pairs only with T and G pairs only with C. The members of the pairs are joined to each other by chemical bonds, and then the two free ends are

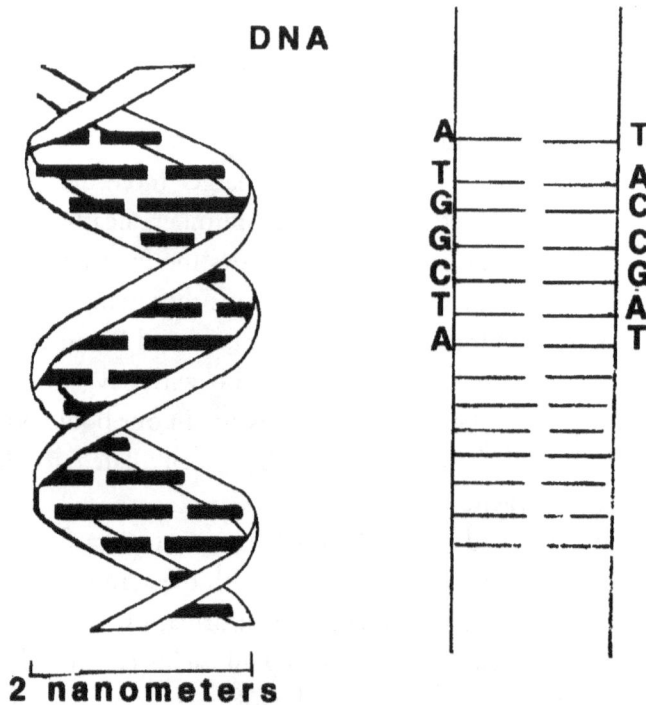

DNA

2 nanometers

Figure 22

bonded each to a sugar-phosphate backbone. The two backbones wind together in a "double helix" which resembles a spiral staircase. The first step of the stairway may be A+T, the second G+C and so on. The sequence of bases in the gene governs the configuration of a protein. Our bodies consist of muscle and tissue protein (think of a thick steak) and other substances the manufacture of which is controlled by enzymes. Enzymes are special proteins that catalyze chemical reactions in our bodies. As an example, the gene which is responsible for the manufacture of hemoglobin consists of about 438 letters coded into 146 three letter words using the four letter alphabet A,T,G,C. The letter pairs are separated in distance by about 0.33 nanometers (billionths of a meter) and the gene is about twenty nanometers long. See Figure 22.

Normal adult human hemoglobin consists of two different chains of the four nitrogenous bases A, G, C, T. The two chains are called alpha and beta. Human and gorilla alpha chains differ by only two substitutions; the beta chains by only one. Does any reader wish to quarrel with Darwin?

So each gene is expressed by a section of the chromosomal double helix DNA. The totality of genes in our bodies is called "the human genome", of which there has been much written in the press as our scientists map the location of all the genes in the genome, an extremely formidable task!

Now for three really remarkable characteristics of DNA; three characteristics which should fill us with wonder and gratitude! As our bodies "live" their cells are constantly replaced, constantly replicating, as the double helix divides where the two bases join; each half is the template for creating two other DNA strands which, upon cell division, form cells identical to the first! Since we can live for a hundred years, this process must preserve the identity of the DNA for that length of time without a mistake! Well, almost, because the second miraculous characteristic is that, rarely, the DNA will suffer a mutation, the substitution of a letter in the chain, (the substitution of one of the four bases) that produces an altered gene. It is this characteristic which provides for changes and improvements in the species.

So, DNA combines stability (100 years +), reproducibility, and the opportunities for gradual change (mutation). Together with Darwinian "natural selection", the improvement of the species is assured, at least in the sense of adaptation to its environment. What an elegant system! Is it just an accident? Why have we been able to decipher these codes and unravel these mysteries? But there is more! Biotechnologists have discovered the tools needed to reconstruct genes in ways that natural mutation hasn't yet discovered! These tools are a "molecular scissors", a group of enzymes which will each seek out a different, particular sequence of bases in a DNA strand

and go snip, snip and cut the DNA strand at the desired location. Next, there is a "molecular glue" which will join strands of DNA to form a host DNA with new genetic sequences. Finally, there is a way to culture and grow by replication a great many clones of a strand of host DNA using host cells of E.coli. So man is able to accelerate the development of the species in directions he chooses, directions that may or may not turn out to be desirable. In this sense one may think of "autoevolution"!

Why is nature so cooperative? Why do we have the ability to understand and use these elegant and sophisticated tools which have the potential to modify all of nature: plants, animals and humans? Can Homo sapiens be trusted with this formidable influence on the future of our species? Like the nuclear genie, the biotech genie needs to be on a leash when he comes out of the bottle! Has this power been bestowed upon us? Or is it a consequence of nature being nature and of us being so smart?

Chapter Seventeen

Clues

We began with a quote from Einstein, "The eternal mystery of the universe is its comprehensibility". We asked the questions: "Does that comprehensibility give us any clues to the Creator's nature or to his purpose?". "If we seek clues will we find evidence that may lead us to surmise that a helpful hand is guiding the evolution of our species?". "Or that it is not?".

Our quest has been far ranging. At times the reader must have wondered why we were exploring the margins of the jungles of mathematics and physics. The reason, of course, is that we were searching for clues, and the clues, if there are any, are embedded in these two subjects. We may have found some! Let's list what we have found.

Clues from the Physical World

When we look about us at the Physical World we see the way the Creator did things, or, does things, or both. Just as an artist's paintings reveal a lot about the nature of the artist, we may expect to see the Creator's works reveal something of the nature of the Creator. The laws of nature must be an expression of *his* nature. What clues confront us in the natural world?

The First Clue—The Big Bang.

Our magnificent universe began with the Big Bang; it was created from an immense quantity of energy in a tiny package. Can we hope to comprehend anything of this magnitude? Yes! Thanks to the gifts of our big brains and mathematics we find the universe comprehensible! The Big Bang and its echoes, which surround us, leave no doubt that we and the universe are here because of a creative event. That evidence is very powerful. Our convictions about causality, cause and effect, convince us that there is, or was, a source of some sort responsible for that event. We search for that source. Newton said, "We have explained the phenomena of planetary motion by the power of gravity, but we have not yet assigned the cause of this power." A similar statement applies to the origin of the universe. Unsatisfied with our ignorance we say "God", but while that may satisfy some, it leaves us none the wiser. **We remain ignorant of the Creator, but the Big Bang is evidence of the Creator's presence at that time.**

The Second Clue—The Reliability of the Natural Laws.

The Natural Laws never change, or, at least, the evidence is that they have not changed since the Big Bang. We depend on these laws for our very existence. We depend on gravity to keep us pinned to the surface of our planet; gravity never changes. We depend on the continuing radiation from the sun. As we look back toward the beginning of our universe the light that left its source star billions of years ago has the same characteristics as the light we generate today, here on earth, in our atomic plasmas. The velocity with which the light travels through empty space is the same for every photon. The mass and charge of an electron is the same for every electron. These are things we can count on. We take these things for granted. We believe the natural laws will continue to act in the future as they have in the past. **The stability and reliability of the natural laws provide for our continued existence. We are persuaded that the source is there still, still in control.**

The Third Clue—The Synergy Between Nature and Mathematics.

Einstein asked, "How can it be that mathematics, being after all a product of human thought independent of experience, is so admirably adapted to the objects of reality?". The entire body of mathematics is self-consistent and can be pursued independently of nature; but math *is* the means by which we understand nature, predict its behavior, and control it to our benefit. **Why does the universe "fit" mathematical description so elegantly?**

Which came first, math or nature? A modern engineer would surmise that this chicken and egg question would have to be resolved in favor of mathematics because mathematics is independent of the natural world. It had to come first! Mathematics set the design standard! Some believe that math *must* be an expression of the Creator's nature. Things are the way they are because that's the way the Creator wants it, or wanted it. Much of what we've learned about math we have learned as a consequence of our attempts to understand nature, the nature he created. Math appeared on our radar screen only recently, in the last 10,000 years. As a consequence of math, Homo sapiens' relation to nature has changed dramatically. Instead of being subject to nature's whims, Homo sapiens now uses math to control nature. Why does math resonate so profoundly with nature? There is a remarkable synergistic relationship between nature and math; might they be derived from the same source, to have a common origin? **Are math and nature both a reflection of the Creator's nature?**

The Fourth Clue—Nature's Obedience to a Few General Laws.

Maxwell's equations, the wave equation, Schrodinger's equation, the laws of gravitation, the laws of Relativity, the laws of probability, natural selection, a few fundamental mathematical forms encompass the laws of the universe. **Why is our complex world readily explained by a few general laws, relatively simple general laws?** Einstein spent the last portion of his life searching for a "Unified Theory", based on mathematics, that would knit all the pieces of natural law into a single whole. Clearly, this brilliant man expected a single concept to underlie all of nature. He did not find it. Physicists continue to search for it today; they call it T.O.E., The Theory of Everything! Perhaps there is no unifying theory. Perhaps, there is, but like atomic and nuclear knowledge, the next level of comprehension may reveal forces so terrifying that we are not yet ready for that revelation.

The Fifth Clue—The Pyramid of Complexity

The natural world has been configured in such a way that simplicity is at the foundation of a very complex world. Because of this structure it has been possible for man to build his knowledge of nature beginning with simple models and then, as his experimental explorations revealed new knowledge, to progress to the sophisticated and complex. First we understood our solar system, then our galaxy, then the cosmos. First we understood the simple hydrogen atom, then the helium atom, then all the elements up to the most complex. First we understood the characteristics of visible light, then the dual nature of light waves and particles and the extension to tiny particles of matter. **Is this pyramidal characteristic of the natural world, which has been so beneficial to man, an accident of creation, or does some intent lie behind it?**

The Sixth Clue—The role of Chance

Chance is at work everywhere in the natural world: mutation and the evolution of species, the laws that govern the tiny world of the atom and the nucleus, the chance that governs the conception of each new human being. **Chance provides for certainty on the macroscopic scale and for change at the microscopic scale. Is this a glimpse into the mind of the Creator?**

Clues from the Non-physical World

No intelligent, educated person will quarrel with evolution. The evidence for this theory is all around us. The Creator built evolution into his set of rules for the universe. The real question which confronts us is not Creationism in the biblical sense; it is **INTERVENTION.** We have "free will", but while free will precludes intervention in our personal decisions it does not seem to preclude intervention in the natural world.

Some people in the past collection of Homo sapiens were possessed of remarkable gifts. In the world of math and physics such names as Archimedes, Newton, Gauss, Maxwell and Einstein rush to our minds. Are their remarkable gifts, or their discoveries, evidence of intervention? If there was such intervention, is that a violation of man's free will? No, these individuals were still free to make their own choices; free to use or ignore their enormous gifts. In the same way, intervention in the natural world with the intent to influence the *opportunities* for man's development, to present him with choices he might otherwise not have, would not seem to rob him of free will. If the Creator has a continuing interest in Homo sapiens; if that "benign hand" is giving us a nudge occasionally, we should see some clues.

As we look about us and at history do we see any improbable events that may make us suspect intervention? Let's look at the evidence.

The First Clue—The Selection of Homo sapiens.

Does it not seem strange that Homo sapiens exists on the planet as the only representative of the human condition? Does it make sense that our closest relative in the natural domain appears to be the chimpanzee? There is no creature nearly as close to Homo sapiens as is the donkey to the horse! Why did Eve play the role she played? What were her special gifts to all of us? Why have the other derivatives of Homo erectus all vanished? The

Neanderthals were survivors of the first rank and there were many of them; why are they gone and we are here? Is it just a curious accident of history?

The Second Clue—The Synergy between Our Capabilities and the Natural World.

Why is the nature we encounter on our planet so kind to us? Would a desert planet or one covered with ice have done as well? Nature is very accommodating; the temperatures, abundance of water, exploitable natural resources and other conditions under which we exist and prosper seem to have been designed for us! Or have we been designed by natural selection for planet earth's conditions, as Darwin might insist? Which is it? Or may these be two sides to the same coin?

Our brain-size, our opposed thumb and our ability to form speech all distinguish us from other animals. We are unique! These unique characteristics have enabled us to develop the tools needed to understand and control the natural world. Why is man *so* different from all other animals? Why are we the only kind of creature on the planet to exhibit these abilities? Was Homo sapiens selected by a cosmic design to survive when all other subsets of Homo erectus failed? Or was the selection Darwinian, natural? Those who would attempt to untangle this mystery face a very challenging task.

The Third Clue—The American Experience

As one ponders the history of the New World and the American experience it becomes more and more puzzling. One wonders if there might be evidence of cosmic intervention.

Fifty thousand years ago Homo sapiens dwelled in some region of southeastern Africa and from there spread out over the planet. The last of the continents he journeyed to were North and South America. The travelers to the New World crossed the Bering Strait during the Ice Age; before there was any math or science. As the Ice Age did its meltdown the seas rose and closed the Strait behind them, the travelers were isolated in the Americas. Was this isolation part of a plan?

Math and science appear to have originated more-or-less independently in Egypt, in the Fertile Crescent, in India, and in China. Although there was some communication among these areas, it was very meager. In the beginning, cross-fertilization in these two subjects was undoubtedly almost inconsequential. So math and science sprang up and flourished independently in these isolated societies, but not to any significant degree in the Americas.

The Incas, the Aztecs and the Mayans were large and prosperous societies; their buildings and art demonstrate a high level of sophistication. Why was there no significant math and science? There is no logical reason to believe that these peoples could not have developed, in their isolation, beyond even the level achieved in Europe. Had these peoples developed a math and science equal to or better than the Europeans' they might well have been able to deny the Americas to the European invaders. But was this contrary to some cosmic intent?

The most desirable part of the two continents in terms of temperature, water, fertile soil and natural resources was ignored because the indigenous population had no gold. And this natural Eden was the most poorly defended. The primitive indigenous people in what is now the United States were a collection of individual tribes seldom capable of joint defense. This situation created an island of opportunity for the northern Europeans. Then, when the Europeans came, why were the emigrants from England, with their concepts of individual freedom and equality under the law, the ones to dominate the settlement of what is now the United States? Their new paradigm for freedom and self-government attracted swarms of Europeans who built the new republic into the most powerful on the planet and made it the leader in world affairs. An accident? Think about it!

The Fourth Clue—The Flood of Knowledge.

There is an ever increasing surge of knowledge which carries us forward in our understanding of the universe: mathematics, electric, magnetic and gravitational fields, the structure of atoms and the structure of ourselves, our evolution, our DNA. Those of us who inhabit our planet today contribute to that flood, that broadening river, but its purpose remains a mystery. Why are we the beneficiaries of all this knowledge? Why has it appeared so recently in human history? Some may say that the Creator wants us to have it, but WHY? If this conjecture has some validity, why should he want us to have it? **Is this cornucopia of knowledge evidence that there is some purpose guiding us in some unknown direction toward some unknown destination?**

Clues from the mathematical world

Mathematics

Starting with a row of beans, Homo sapiens has developed the entire intellectual world of mathematics! Apart from its utility as a means to understand and quantify natural phenomena, mathematics has other-worldly properties of a very mysterious nature; one would just not expect a row of beans to invoke such a complex and sophisticated world. The dual nature of "e" and pi, both having a relationship with nature and with the purely intellectual realm of math, and the parallel duality of waves and particles must intrigue us enormously. **These are mysteries of the first rank, and, perhaps, insights into the mind of the Creator.**

The men and women to whom we owe our knowledge of math were a very select group; they were endowed with powerful intellects of a special kind. Most are little known by the general public. For the most part they were consumed by their subject; it was a passion, not a livelihood. Many overcame obstacles of poverty or parents who were either indifferent to their brilliance or who actually stood in their way. On the other hand, many found mentors who assisted them as they developed their potential. Were they and their mentors selected by the Creator to provide this marvelous gift to their fellows?

Once there is a row of beans and then a number system all of math follows! Math is an enormous subject; a subject of which we have probably barely scratched the surface. Why is mathematics the way it is? Math is independent of nature. Math is eternal. If the Creator is eternal, then math and its complex intricacies must be a reflection of his nature! **The great gift to man is not mathematics; it is man's ability to understand mathematics, the ability to discover and understand the eternal.** Why does Homo sapiens have the ability to develop and use this marvelous set of procedures? **Can it be other than an enormous gift from the Creator?**

Occam's Razor

Each of these clues is thought-provoking, and each reader must make his or her own judgement of the significance of these clues. Are they just curious threads that form the warp of our historical tapestry or are they more; do they give us insights into the nature of the Creator? The reader may wish to take advantage of the wisdom of a 14th century philosopher and logician named William Occam. Occam was born in Surrey, England, entered the Franciscan Order, taught at Oxford University, was denounced by Pope John XXII and died in Munich of the plague. Occam the logician proposed a guide known as Occam's Razor for those considering alternative solutions for philosophical problems: "Entities are not to be multiplied without necessity". A more understandable restatement might be: "When considering the alternative explanations for phenomena, the simplest alternative often turns out to be the best choice".

At the end of our journey we find a set of clues and Occam's Razor. What will be the result of applying the Razor to our clues? Are those clues substantial; will the Razor reply, "Of course!"? Or will the Razor say, "Wishful thinking!".

WHAT DO YOU THINK?

Epilogue

We may or may not have identified clues and insights into the Creator's nature, but, in any case, we have found no clue to the answer to the question "Why are we here"? Why was there a creative event, a Big Bang? Why do the natural laws appear to be eternal? Why do we continue to survive? Are we a part of the rationale for creation or are we just an accident of the architecture of the universe? Is our evolution only a chance byproduct of the natural laws that govern the universe? Or, as some of us choose to think, are we the sole reason for that creative event! Is there any justification for that opinion? Was our evolution programmed into the paradigm from the beginning? The fact of the matter is, of course, that we don't know. We sit here on our tiny planet, illuminated by a mediocre star, part of an undistinguished spiral galaxy; what justification do we have for believing we are not just a chance occurrence in an immense universe? Let's review the evidence.

We have evidence that we are probably all descended from one woman, Eve. This is a truly remarkable occurrence. Can it have happened by chance? We know that at one time our genus, Homo sapiens, cohabited the planet with several other sub-species of Homo erectus. Those sub-species are gone and we are here, and we don't know why. Was it only chance? We know that our brains have evolved from chimp-size to our size; with a sudden inflation in size about 500,000 years ago, the cause of which is unknown to us. Some believe it was a change in diet that triggered the inflation, but there is a large speculative factor in that surmise. We don't know why. Was the inflation due solely to natural causes?

Africa appears to be our continent of origin. About 50,000 years ago, in Africa, there was a spectacular advance in language, art and social behavior, but we don't know what caused it. Was it just chance? About the same time our ancestors migrated from Africa to Europe, Asia and Australia. Why were they motivated to leave familiar surroundings and venture into a strange and potentially dangerous new environment? Why did their new home in the Orient, Near East and Europe become the cradle of mathematics and science? Would it have happened anyway if they had chosen to remain in southeastern Africa?

Homo sapiens' understanding of the natural world began and then progressed with his increasing knowledge of mathematics. The beginning of math was tallying; the first monumental discovery was a number system. There was a burst of mathematical discovery in ancient Mesopotamia, Egypt and Greece followed by modest progress in the Orient and nearly two thousand years of intellectual darkness in Europe. Why was there such a long period of stagnation? The sun arose again in the seventeenth century and there was an explosion of progress. Numbers were found to have mysterious properties. Analytic geometry, the calculus, combinatorial analysis and the laws of chance were discovered. Math is not a property of the physical world; why did Homo sapiens discover it? Was the discovery of math inevitable? Or was it a gift?

The application of math to analyzing physical phenomena accompanied the rebirth of experimentation; Galileo picked up the experimental flag where Pythagorous had dropped it two millennia before. Tools and instruments: the telescope, the microscope, the mechanical clock and the magnetic compass encouraged exploration of the cosmos, the miniscule and the planet. The Inquisition faltered and disappeared, run out of town by reason and knowledge. The "natural philosophers" began to pursue and capture the laws of nature.

The mathematicians and scientists of the seventeenth, eighteenth, nineteenth and twentieth centuries made enormous progress. They explored the cosmos, the atom, the nucleus of the atom, the human genome, the gravitational and electromagnetic fields, the relativistic structure of time and our universe. Reason replaced superstition.

Why? Why, after millions of years of human habitation of this planet, was there this sudden appearance of Homo sapiens and a related explosion of learning and knowledge? Was it just an accident?

Do we Homo sapiens have a mission for which we are being prepared; for which we are being educated? Is this the reason for that river of knowledge? Do we Homo sapiens resonate with the will of a power we can not identify but which we continue to search for? Are the great religions of history and of today a manifestation of that resonance? As we become more rational in our behavior and in our thought processes will we begin to see a destiny that is now hidden from us?

If, as genus Homo sapiens, we are to accomplish a mission, how will we discover what the mission is and what preconditions we must satisfy? If there is such a mission in our future, a mission which must involve all of mankind, then, certainly, a high priority must be given to tranquil relations within the genus. War and ethnic conflict do not lead to tranquility and a cooperative effort across all of humankind. Before we can be trusted as a genus with any mission we must first learn to manage ourselves.

Linus Pauling, a very brilliant scientist and humanist, winner of two Nobel Prizes, one in science and the second a peace award, expressed the hope that politicians and others outside the scientific disciplines would learn to apply the rational thought-procedures of science to their realms of influence. Einstein and other leading figures who possessed both great intelligence and great knowledge are numbered among the peace-makers. Men of great intelligence and knowledge do not make aggressive war; they recognize that in wars everyone loses. However, when the barbarians are at the gates men and women of good conscience must defend themselves and their values.

What has history shown us regarding the conditions which lead to tranquility among men? Some of the great religions admonish us to "love one another", but that admonition has not done the job. Tranquility among our fellows seems to flourish in an atmosphere of comfort, intelligence and knowledge. We lead more comfortable, satisfying and rewarding lives when we have plenty to eat, adequate shelter, an education, interesting and challenging work and leisure to pursue our interests. In this kind of atmosphere competition leads to progress in a climate of courteous and considerate interpersonal relations. It appears that our planet has the resources to provide a comfortable life for all its inhabitants if those resources are carefully and intelligently utilized. But will intelligence, knowledge, courtesy and kindness ultimately prevail?

Knowledge is increasing and spreading across the planet at such a rapid rate that we should soon be able to provide for the needs of all. The path to this kind of utopian planet is the path of intelligence, knowledge and cooperation. Some people are on that path and are moving down the path at an accelerating rate. Others choose a path of ethnic conflict; some choose personal aggrandizement at the expense of their fellows; some say let the devil take the hindmost; some prefer to stand aside and watch. Who will prevail?

As we look back in history, we are able to assign natural causes to many, even most, but not all, of the transitions in Homo sapiens' evolution. That's the **what.** We don't know the **why!** We are searching for the catalyst that may have enabled those transitions. We are searching for the reason things are the way they are. We have learned much about managing nature, but we know little about its most fundamental secrets. We have yet to learn *why* nature is the way it is. There is one school that replies, "If things were not as they are we would not be here to ask the question!" True, but that conclusion leaves the question unanswered!

Do we have a destiny as a genus? Is there a future mission for Homo sapiens? Are we to be a successful experiment? Is there a Creator who has an interest in us?

Many mysteries confront us, many unanswered questions. To some, the evidence that there is a Creator continuing to function in our universe is very powerful. The evidence that there may be a benign force at work on our behalf is circumstantial, but there seems to be much circumstantial evidence. Many find comfort in that evidence. In this book we have attempted to examine some of that evidence in an effort to determine if there **is** a guiding hand interested in our future. Have we made any progress toward that goal?

HAVE WE SEEN THE THUMBPRINT?

Appendix One

The differential equation for the growth of bacteria, rabbits and other similar populations is:

$$dR/dt = kR$$

(Here the slash mark / indicates that the quantity before the slash is divided by the quantity following the slash). Now, dR/dt is the time rate of population increase, R is the population at time t, k is a constant of proportionality. The expression "dR/dt" says: Let dR be a very tiny change in the population that takes place in a very tiny time dt. Then dR/dt is the instantaneous Rate of population change at that time. The instantaneous rate is so many rabbits (dR) per second (dt). That rate is proportional to the number of rabbits R present at that time. The ratio dR/dt increases as the rabbit production continues. Refer to Fig. 23.

RABBIT POPULATION GROWTH

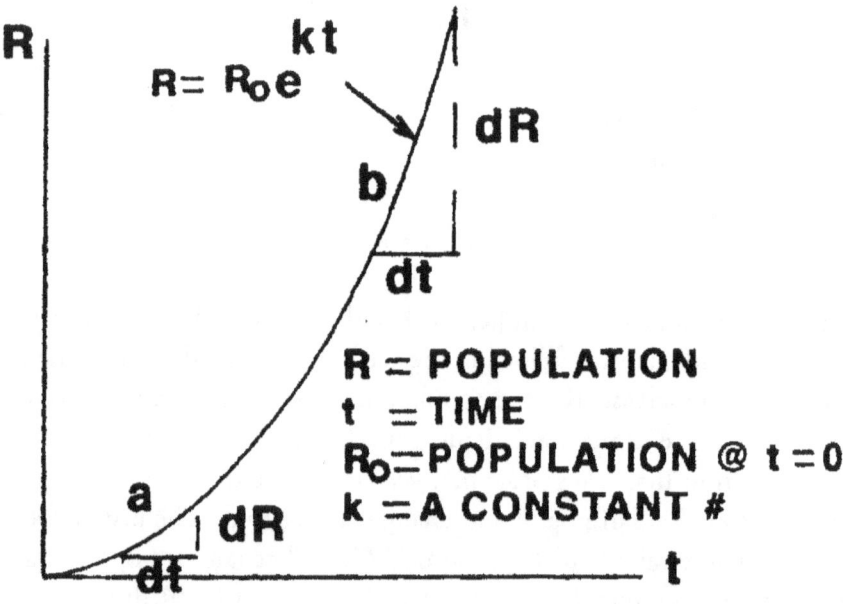

Figure 23

At area b of the curve of Fig. 23 dR is twice as large as it was at area a, while the size of dt is the same at both a and b. Therefore the ratio at area b is about twice that of area a since dt is the same size at both a and b. The rate of increase of R is increasing, the slope of the curve is becoming steeper.

Now let's solve the equation. Multiply both sides of the equation by dt/R and cancel terms which are the same in numerator and denominator on the expression on each side of the equals sign :

$$dR/dt(dt/R) = kR(dt/R);$$

canceling terms that appear in both numerator and denominator of each expression:dR/R = kdt

Now we "integrate" both sides:
$$\ln R = kt + \text{constant}$$

Where did that equation come from? It comes from a freshman college course in calculus. (If you never had freshman calculus, and never saw integration before, don't worry about it. If you worry about it excessively, then you'll have to take a course in calculus).

That last equation has another form:

$R = e^{kt + \text{constant}}$ (This comes from the same college course).

We rewrite the equation one more time:

$R = R_0 e^{kt}$ where R_0 has replaced the constant term e^{constant}

Now this may look like a lot of rabbits coming out of the hat to some readers. Be reassured. If you are ignorant of the necessary calculus to follow the solution you are in the same situation as a person, such as the author, who, when asked to name the capital of Lithuania, had to seek help from his World Atlas (The capital is Vilnius). Ignorance is not a sin. It can be corrected by reference to a world atlas or a course in calculus..

This rabbit-growth equation is a typical example of the type of equation solved by the calculus in that it involves a RATE.

A second very important quantity is $e^{-kt} = 1/e^{kt}$. Now, as kt becomes large e^{-kt} becomes very small. Picture a very large reservoir of water that is filling a small, deep vessel with water through a pipe located at the bottom of the smaller vessel. The top of the small vessel is a few inches higher than the water level in the reservoir. At first there is a large differential in the heights of the liquid in the two vessels and the water flows freely. Then, as the water level in the small vessel approaches the level of the water in the large reservoir, the rate of flow becomes smaller and smaller until the water ceases to flow when the two liquid levels are the same. This is what happens in the electrical circuits of your TV when you turn it on; at first the electrons flow very rapidly as they "charge up" the components; then the electrons slow and cease to flow as the charge up is completed.

Appendix Two

Exponents and Logarithms

If we are to talk about exponential processes we must know what an exponent is, and we have to become comfortable with the concept of the base in a number system.

When mathematicians write 2x2x2x2, two multiplied by itself four times, they use a shorthand 2^4. If the number they are dealing with is 2^{100}, two multiplied by itself 100 times, the shorthand certainly saves a lot of effort and paper. Mathematicians have named the 4 and the 100 in these two examples "exponents", and 2 is known as the "base".

Indeed, even today, the computer, cornerstone of the Information Revolution, depends on the base two: on/off, or zeros and ones in mathematical jargon. Of course, the transistors don't know a one from a hole in the ground (a zero), all they know is their twofold state, ON or OFF. (Can we count beyond two without finding new symbols and number-words; without the number three? Indeed we can, and do, many thousands of times a second in our computers where the number sequence is based on a pair of symbols, ones and zeros, the equivalents of ON/OFF: 01,10,11,100,...(a code for 1,2,3,4,...), a number system based on two. The genetic code in human genes is based on a sequence of two pairs of chemicals, very similar in principle to computer code.

The base doesn't have to be two, it can be any number. Sixteen is a convenient base in computer software. The decimal base we all use is ten. 10^2

is 100, ten multiplied by itself twice. Notice that the exponent "2", the superscript number adjacent to 10, identifies the number of zeros in 100. What exponent would you associate with100,000 which has five zeros? The exponent would be five of course:

$$10^5 = 100,000$$

Now, if we multiply 1000x100 = 10^3 x 10^2 =100,000 we see that adding the two exponents together gives us 10^5 which we just learned is 100,000. A mathematical operation of multiplication has been replaced by one of adding exponents. This is what is meant by "logarithms". Tables of logarithms have been prepared which greatly simplify multiplication of large numbers. The exponents need not be whole numbers; they may be decimal numbers. For example 3.3010 is the logarithm of 2,000. i.e. 2000=$10^{3.3010}$ (This can be rewritten 2000 = $10^{(3 + 0.3010)}$) The number to the left of the decimal sign in the exponent (3) identifies the integer power of ten, in this case 10^3 or 1000. The integer power of ten is then multiplied by the number corresponding to the decimal power of ten (0.3010), in this case $10^{0.3010}$ which equals 2. So $10^{3.3010}$ = 1000x2 = 2000.

To multiply any two numbers one looks up the logarithm of each, one adds them, and then finds their sum in the table and the corresponding product.

For example, if we look at a table of logarithms we find that the logarithm to the base ten of 5 is 0.6990, that is to say, $10^{0.6990}$ = 5. In the same way, the logarithm of 2 is 0.3010 i.e. $10^{0.3010}$ = 2. In order to multilply two by five we add these two logarithms:

0.6990 + 0.3010 = 1.000. We know that 1 is the logarithm for 10, 10^1 = 10, the correct value for the product of 2 and 5.

Division is done similarly by subtraction of logarithms.

Logarithms were a great advance in ease of calculation involving very large numbers; they were *discovered* by a Scottish laird named John Napier in 1614 and subsequently improved by others.

Appendix Three

The Properties of "e"

How does one calculate this remarkable number e? There are various ways. The first one we shall consider is:

$$e=(1+1/n)^n \text{ when n becomes infinitely large.}$$

Let's calculate an approximate value for "e" when n=3. We won't come very close to the right answer because the formula gives the right answer only for n infinitely large; but let's see what we get:

$$e=(1+ 1/3)^3$$

The exponent n=3 tells us to multiply one and one-third by itself three times:

$$e=4/3 \times 4/3 \times 4/3 = 64/27 = 2.37\ldots.$$ clearly, a small value of n gives a poor approximation to the correct value of 2.718....

Now let's try n=10.

$$e=(1+ 1/10)^{10}$$

$1.1 \times 1.1 \times 1.1 \times 1.1 \times 1.1 \times 1.1 \times 1.1 \times 1.1 \times 1.1 \times 1.1 = 2.594$ using four place logarithms: Logarithm of 1.1=0.0414; 0.0414x10=0.414; number corresponding to logarithm 0.414=2.594

2.594 is an improvement on 2.37, but still not very close to 2.718...

As we expected, this approximate value for e is not very close to the correct value of 2.718…We can correctly infer from this that a very large value of n is needed to find a close approximation to the actual number for e.

The second formula we shall consider is:
$$e=1+1/1!+1/2!+1/3!+1/4!+1/5! +…$$
where the dots indicate that the series of numbers continues in this pattern forever. What is the meaning of (!) in this series? Mathematicians use a lot of shorthand; we've just seen an example where exponents provide a shorthand for showing the same number multiplied by itself many times (10^5=10x10x10x10x10). The exclamation mark in the last formula for e is shorthand; the shorthand says that N! means the number N is multiplied by all the positive integers greater than zero and less than N. For example if N=3, 3!=3x2x1=6, if N=5, 5!=5x4x3x2x1=120, etc.

In the second formula, calculate an approximate value for "e" using the first five terms of the series:
$$e= 1+1/1!+1/2!+1/3!+1/4! = 1+1+1/2+1/6+1/24=2.701.$$

This calculation for e is much better than the first formula, that is to say, closer to the correct value, but clearly very many terms are required for a close approximation to the actual value of 2.7182818….

As we discussed earlier, approximations are very important when we are dealing with the problems we must solve in the practical world of industry and commerce. These calculations for "e" are good examples of the use of approximations. If our analysis of some problem can be satisfied with an answer that has a sizeable error, but is good enough for our purposes, we can use 2.701 for a value of e, we need not use a terribly exact value such as 2.7182818284590…(Richard Feynman, a brilliant physicist and Nobel laureate, once told his class that during the development of the atomic bomb one of the scientists at Los Alamos came to him for help in finding the sum of an infinite series "in closed form", that is to say, the exact sum. Feynman asked him, "How exact must the number be?". When the man answered, Feynman told him to add the first ten terms in the series and that sum would be sufficiently accurate for his needs! The bomb development moved forward based on an approximate number.)

The second of the formulas we used to calculate the value of e is known as an infinite series because there is no limit to the number of terms; the series of terms 1/n! continues forever. There are many of these infinite series and they are extremely useful for both theoretical math and also for calculation. If a solution to a problem can be found in the form of a series it is necessary only to add terms to acquire an approximate numerical value. Mathematicians have found other infinite series that are very useful, for example the infinite series for:

$$e^x = 1 + x/1! + x^2/2! + x^3/3! + \ldots.$$

With x=1 we see e = 1+ 1+ 1/2! +1/3! +.... just as we found it in the second formula for e above.

Appendix Four

Euler's Famous Formula

We begin with a mathematician named De Moivre who is usually associated with the discovery of the following famous equation:

$$e^{ia} = \text{cosine } a + i \text{ sine } a$$

Pause for a moment and become acquainted with DeMoivre's equation.

(This equation is the key to the arcane formula which we shall get to shortly). In De Moivre's equation a is an angle, cosine a and sine a are as shown in Fig. 24 and "i" is a symbol for the square root of-1, that is to say (i) x (i) =-1; "ia" is an exponent and e is the natural base. It is important to recognize that i is just another number; it is not a number that can be put into correspondence with a bean or a pebble; but neither is the number zero and we have become comfortable with zero. We are uncomfortable with i only because it is unfamiliar.

ANGLES, SINES AND COSINES

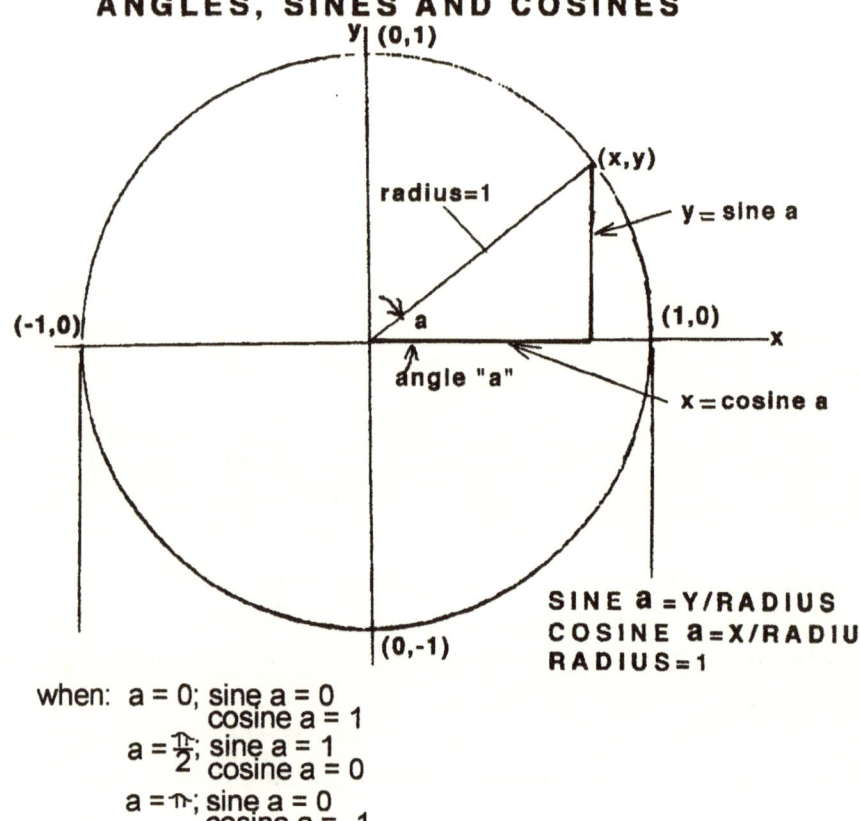

Figure 24

Think about it. Our numbers are 1,2,3,4,5,6,7,8,9, 0, i. i is just a symbol like the other ten. Get used to it!

Before we proceed to Leonard Euler's famous formula a little preparation is in order. Please refer to Fig. 24 which shows a circle drawn at the center of a Cartesian coordinate system. The circle's radius is one (unity). Imagine that a point on this circle travels round the circumference of the circle at a constant speed, just like the ball on a roulette wheel. The coordinates of the traveling point will be x,y and will, of course, change as the point travels round the circle. If we start the motion at the point on the circle where x=1 and y=0, and the circular motion proceeds in a sense opposite to the sense in which the hands of a clock move, the value of x will first decrease and the value of y will increase until after a quarter turn x=0 and y=1. Another quarter turn and x=-1, y=0; one more quarter turn and y=-1, x=0, and the next quarter turn brings us back to the starting point x=1, y=0.

As the point continues around the circumference of the circle, the value of x cycles between 1 and-1; a point on the x axis vertically below the traveling point on the circle goes back and forth, back and forth between 1 and-1. The point on the x axis travels fastest midway between 1 and-1. As it crosses zero it gradually slows down and then reverses at the end points of its travel.

Suppose now that the point moving along the x axis carries a pencil and that paper from a long roll is moving with constant speed in the y direction beneath the pencil point. The pencil point will draw a sinuous-looking (Webster: sinuous = wavy) curve on the paper like Fig. 25.

SINUSOIDAL WAVE GENERATION

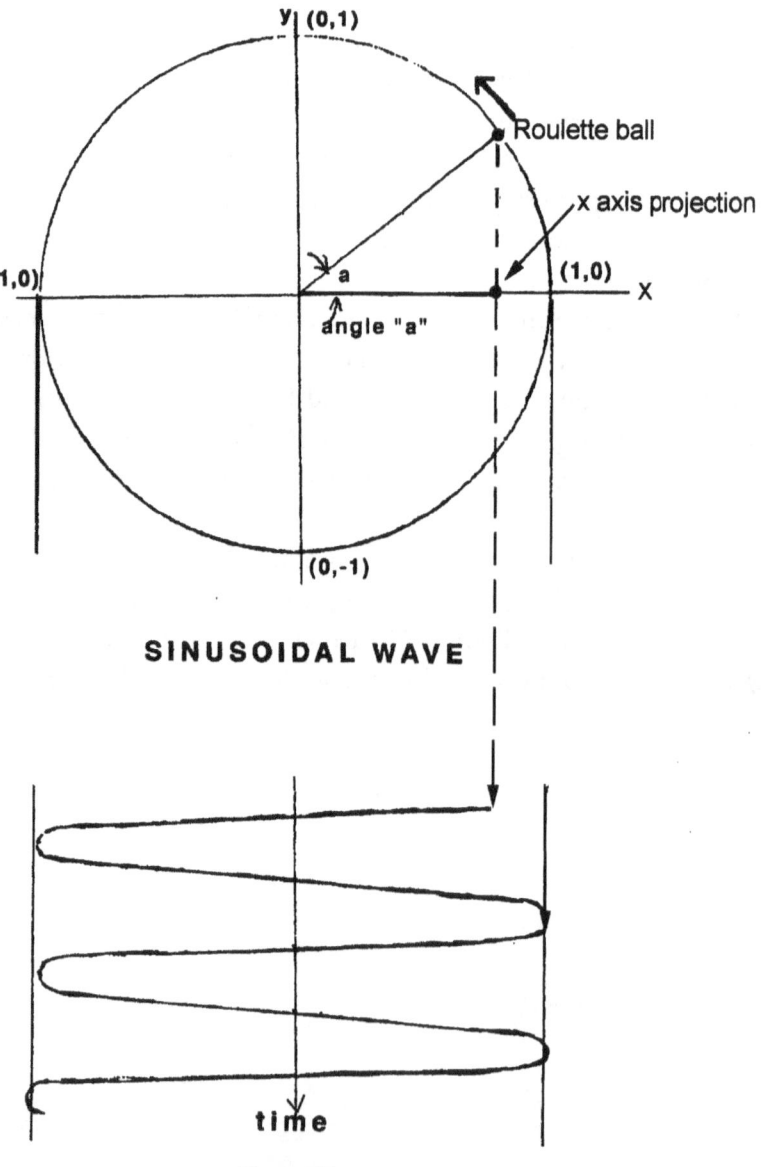

Figure 25

For reasons that are now perfectly clear to us, mathematicians call this a "sinusoidal" wave.

Of course, a point on the y axis behaves in a similar fashion as the point on the x axis except that it reaches its maximum and minimum values a quarter turn later than the point on the x axis.

Look again at Fig.24. Draw a line parallel to the y axis from a point (x,y) on the circle toward the x axis. The line will intersect the x axis at a distance x from the y axis and the length of the line is y. Together with the radius of length 1 a right triangle is formed with angle "a" formed by the base (x) of the triangle and the radius (r). In such a right triangle mathematicians have named the ratio of the length of the side opposite angle "a" (the side is "y" in our example) to the hypotenuse (the radius in our example) the "sine" of the angle "a". Sine a = y/r. The ratio is y/1 because y is the length of the side opposite "a" and we have chosen the length of the radius equal to 1. Likewise the ratio of the side adjacent to angle "a" (x in our example) to the hypoteneuse (the radius in our example) is called the "cosine". That ratio, cosine a = x/1. If the point (x,y) has moved to x =-1, y = 0 then the cosine is-1 and the sine is 0.

Remember the values for sine (0) and cosine (-1) when the angle "a" is pi radians (180 degrees) because we shall use that information shortly. Reread this section, study the figure for a moment and it will all make sense.

One more important fact, mathematicians must work with numbers and in the real world those numbers are often ratios. Angles in math are not usually expressed in degrees, but as the ratio of the length of a portion of a circle's circumference to the length of its radius. That ratio is a number. The ratios that are used to express angular measure are called radians. When the portion of the circumference is the same length as the length of the radius of the circle the ratio is one and the angle is called one radian; one radian equals approximately 57.3 degrees. See Fig. 26.

ANGULAR MEASURE IN RADIANS

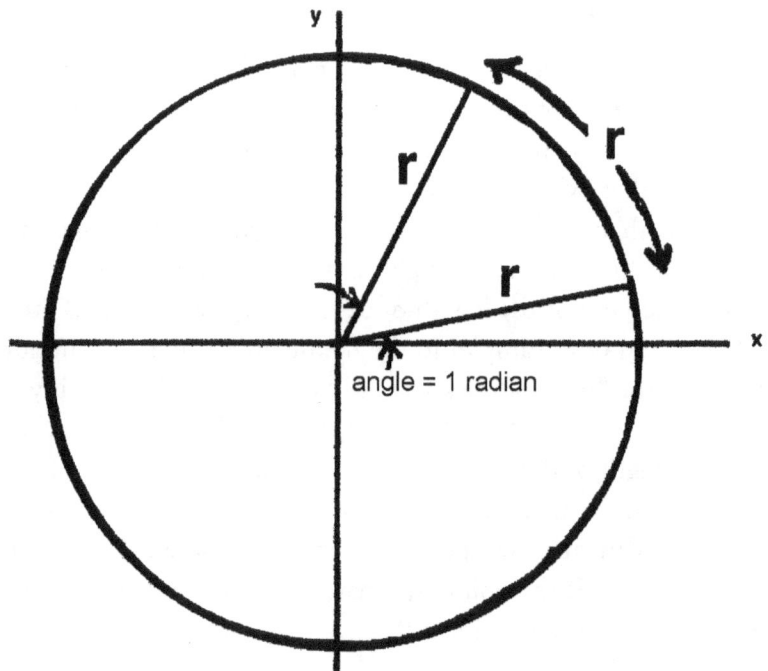

**pi/2 radians per quadrant
pi radians per cemicircle
2 pi radians per circle
one radian=57 degrees**

Figure 26

Remember that pi is the ratio of the circumference of a circle to its diameter. (Pi = circumference/diameter). Since the circumference is pi x diameter = pi x twice the radius, the ratio of the circumference to the radius of the circle is 2pi radians. In more familiar circular measure the associated angle in degrees is 360 degrees. Half way around is pi radians, or 180 degrees. One quarter way around is pi/2 radians or 90 degrees. Radians and degrees are just two different measures for angles in the same way that feet and yards are two different measures for distance.

Euler's formula follows from DeMoivre's equation: when the point on our circle has traveled to the position x =-1 then the angle a equals pi radians (180 degrees) cosine a =-1 and sine a = 0; therefore i x sine pi = 0. (See Figure 24.)

Let's write down DeMoivre's equation for angle a = pi:
$$e^{(i)pi} = \text{cosine pi} + i \text{ sine pi} = -1 + 0$$

This is Euler's Famous Formula: $e^{pi(i)}$ =-1 Refer back to the main text for a discussion of the mysteries related to this famous formula.

Appendix Five

What does the wave equation look like?

$$d^2y/dt^2 = k(d^2y/dx^2)$$

That's pretty intimidating, isn't it? Not really, what it says in mathematical symbols, in the terminology of calculus chosen by our old friend Liebniz, is that the rate of change of the rate of change of y (the wave height) with respect to time, t, equals some constant number, k, times the rate of change of the rate of change of y (the wave height) with respect to distance, x.

Let's simplify that statement. In our automobile, the rate of change of distance with time is velocity, and the rate of change of velocity with time is acceleration. In other words, acceleration is the rate of change of a rate of change. We all know what acceleration in our automobile is, it pushes us back against our seats. Advertisers say "zero to sixty in six seconds"; our forward velocity keeps increasing as we accelerate. And we've all felt an accelerating elevator push us down on the elevator floor. So the term on the left hand side of the equals sign relates to an experience we are all familiar with.

But what is the meaning of the term on the right hand side of the equals sign? If we go at **a constant speed in a horizontal direction**, (the x direction) and climb a mountain where the slope is continually increasing, i.e. the climb is getting steeper and steeper, then the rate of change of the rate of change of our altitude (y) is increasing (accelerating) as our horizontal distance x increases. It is a rate/rate change just like the left side except that distance replaces time. Alright, that is pretty straightforward after a moments stretch of the meninges, but what's the solution to this equation? (Don't try to solve it unless you've had a calculus course in partial differential equations! The solution appears below.) The solution is a wave motion.

If the wave motion is a very pure, simple, endless series of well-behaved wave crests passing by then the solution is:

$$y = A \text{ sine } a(x-vt)$$

where A is the maximum wave height (perhaps a wave five feet high would give the surfer a pleasant ride toward shore) and a is proportional to the frequency with which the wave crests pass a fixed point (perhaps a dozen waves per minute). The wave is travelling to the right in our Cartesian framework. "Frequency" equals the number of wave crests which pass each unit of time (if you receive a phone call every minute the phone call frequency is sixty per hour). The term "sine" is a trigonometric term which simply describes the form of the wave which is illustrated in Fig. 20. Suppose we choose t = 0 in our equation, i.e. t = 0 is the instant at which we start our stopwatch.

then, at that instant: $y = A \text{ sine } ax$

The wave is frozen in time, motionless. If the water were to freeze instantaneously on a wavy day, we would travel from crest to trough to crest to trough as we moved over the ice in the x direction. At that instant the wave amplitude y increases and decreases "sinusoidally" with increasing x. See Fig. 20.

Now choose x = 0, the point at which we are observing.

then $y = A \text{ sine } a(-vt)$

As the time t increases the wave height rises and falls; we bob up and down as we sit on our surfboard located at x = 0.

This, then, is the basic solution for the wave equation that is so common in nature. Complex waveforms can be built up by adding sinusoidal waves of different frequencies. A brilliant mathematician named Fourier developed the math that accomplishes this important result.

Glossary

Analytic Geometry The marriage of algebra and plane geometry.

Atom The smallest quantity of one of the (approximately 100) elements of which nature is composed; further division of the atom discloses atomic elements such as electrons and protons.

Base (1) The quantity of numbers on which a number system is based. In the decimal system the quantity is ten.

Base (2) The nitrogenous chemical bases which carry the information in the genetic code.

Boson A boson belongs to a class of elementary particles which have integral spin (0,1,2,...). Photons are bosons.

Calculus Mathematics based on non-discrete infinitesimal quantities and limiting processes; used to find rates of change and the areas of geometrical figures.

Cell A cell is the fundamental element of living creatures. In humans the cell consists of a nucleus surrounded by a membrane; the nucleus in turn is surrounded by a fluid called the cytoplasm with the nucleus at its center. A confining membrane surrounds the cytoplasm.

Chromosome The key to inherited characteristics. A large DNA molecule which consists of a set of genes.

Complex Number A number consisting of both a real and imaginary part.

Cosine In a right triangle the cosine is the ratio of the side adjacent to a given included angle to the hypotenuse.

Delta Function A geometrical area of infinite height and zero width which enclose a finite area.

DNA The primary genetic material in all organisms. DNA is the format in which all the information required for human functions is expressed. Four nitrogenous bases form the alphabet and "words" which carry the information. These bases occur in pairs joined to each other with the two 'free' ends of the pair joined to the structure of a double helix 'backbone'. The geometry has been compared to a twisted ladder of which the rungs are the paired bases.

Enzyme A protein which catalyzes a metabolic reaction.

Exponent A superscript number which announces the number of times that the quantity of which it is the superscript is multiplied by itself. For example $2^5 = 32$.

Fermions A fermion belongs to a class of elementary particles which have half-integral spin (1/2, 3/2,...). The electron, proton and neutron are fermions.

Gene The unit of inheritance. A section of DNA which encodes a function, usually one protein. Genes reside on chromosomes.

Imaginary Number A number formed by the product of a decimal or integer and the square root of-1.

Integer A whole number, (not a fraction or a decimal number).

Irrational Number A decimal number which can not be expressed as the ratio of two integers.

Molecule The smallest quantity of a substance (there are an enormous number of substances). A molecule is composed of atoms, for example, water molecules contain two hydrogen atoms and one oxygen atom.

Mutation The alteration of the sequences of bases in DNA.

Nanometer One billionth of a meter (10^{-9} meters).

Natural Numbers The set of positive integers which can be placed in a one-to-one correspondence with a row of beans.

Negative Numbers The set of numbers formed by subtracting the positive integers, in succession, from zero.

Positive Numbers The set of numbers formed by successively adding one beginning at zero.

Protein Organic molecules which are required for all life processes.

Quantum A tiny but finite unit amount of energy.

Rational Number A number formed by the ratio of two integers.

Real Number Any decimal number that has no imaginary part.

Set A set is a collection of like objects: the set of prime numbers; the set of citizens of California; the set of trophies of a hunt.

Sine In a right triangle the sine is the ratio of the side opposite a given included angle to the hypotenuse.

Square Root The square root of a given number is that number which when multiplied by itself forms a product equal to the given number.

Wave frequency The number of wave crests which pass a fixed point in unit time.

Wavelength The distance between two wave crests.

About the Author

Born in Huron, South Dakota, February 17, 1922, son of a pioneering physician and his Pennsylvania Dutch wife, John Sewell attended grade school in Huron, secondary school at St. John's Military Academy in Delafield, Wisconsin, and college at MIT in Cambridge, Massachusetts where he was awarded a SB in Electrical Engineering in 1943. He joined the Officer Candidate Program and became an airborne-radar specialist with the Eighth Air Force in WW II. Following three years of service he resumed his education at Cornell University in Ithaca, New York and received a Masters Degree in Physics in 1947.

He spent the next 35 years with the Eastman Kodak Company in Rochester, New York, retired in 1982 as Corporate Vice President and General Manager of the Apparatus Division, an organization of 21,500 hard-working people. He moved to Santa Barbara, California in 1982. Befriended by a Chinese-American man whom he had known at Kodak, Sewell found his way to Silicon Valley and spent the next dozen years associated as a Director with various hi-tech start-up companies. In 1997 he left the Bay Area for Newport Beach and La Quinta, California where he wrote The Eternal Mystery.